Workin... ...n
Seeking...

Also by

R. K. S. Kohli, Social Work with Unaccompanied Asylum Seeking Children*

J. Wade, F. Mitchell, G. Baylis, Unaccompanied Asylum Seeking Children: The Response of Social Work Services

*Also published by Palgrave Macmillan

Working with Unaccompanied Asylum Seeking Children

Issues for Policy and Practice

Ravi K. S. Kohli
and
Fiona Mitchell

palgrave
macmillan

First published in 2007 by
PALGRAVE MACMILLAN
Houndmills, Basingstoke, Hampshire RG21 6XS and
175 Fifth Avenue, New York, N.Y. 10010
Companies and representatives throughout the world.

PALGRAVE MACMILLAN is the global academic imprint of the Palgrave
Macmillan division of St. Martin's Press, LLC and of Palgrave Macmillan Ltd.
Macmillan® is a registered trademark in the United States, United Kingdom
and other countries. Palgrave is a registered trademark in the European
Union and other countries.

ISBN-13: 978–1–4039–9755–5 paperback
ISBN-10: 1–4039–9755–1 paperback
ISBN-13: 978–1–4039–9754–8 hardback
ISBN-10: 1–4039–9754–3 hardback

This book is printed on paper suitable for recycling and made from fully
managed and sustained forest sources. Logging, pulping and manufacturing
processes are expected to conform to the environmental regulations of
the country of origin.

A catalogue record for this book is available from the British Library.

A catalog record for this book is available from the Library of Congress.

10 9 8 7 6 5 4 3 2 1
16 15 14 13 12 11 10 09 08 07

Printed in China

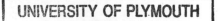

This book is dedicated to unaccompanied children and young people who have to make sense of their place in many worlds as they seek asylum

For Jon Somerton, a good friend and companion, much missed (RK)
For Sam Shearer (FM)

Contents

Notes on Contributors

Judith Dennis is a policy adviser for unaccompanied children at the Refugee Council. She is interested in research looking at refugee protection, particularly for unaccompanied children, and support for children who are not looked after by their parents, especially, how transition to adult life is addressed. She is author of *A Case for Change: How Refugee Children Are Missing Out* (2002) and *Ringing the Changes: The Impact of Guidance on the Use of Sections 17 and 20 of the Children Act 1989 to Support Unaccompanied Asylum-Seeking Children* (2005).

Jo Dixon is a researcher at the Social Work Research and Development Unit, University of York. For the past six years she has been carrying out research into outcomes for care leavers, looked after children and young people on the edge of care. Her research interests include outcomes for vulnerable children and adolescents, leaving care policy and practice and innovative approaches to working with young people in, and at risk of entering, substitute care.

Kimberly Ehntholt is a clinical psychologist at the Lambeth Young Refugee Mental Health Service, South London and Maudsley NHS Trust. She also works at the Traumatic Stress Clinic's Refugee Service, Camden & Islington NHS Trust. Her research interests include developing effective psychological interventions for distressed asylum seekers and refugees, as well as evaluating the impact of immigration detention on children. Recent publications include an article describing a school-based group intervention for war-affected children, as well as a review of effective treatments and strategies for supporting distressed refugee children.

Grace Heaphy is a systemic psychotherapist, currently employed as Academic Tutor on the MSc in Family Therapy Course at the Institute of Psychiatry, Kings College London. She worked in a specialist post for young refugees in Child and Adolescent Mental Services within the South London and Maudsley NHS Foundation Trust for five years until 2006.

Rachel Hek is a lecturer and practice learning manager at the University of Birmingham. She is a qualified social worker and therapist and works independently with children who are looked after. Her research interests are in relation to the services available for refugee and asylum seeking children and their families. Recent publications include: *The Experiences and Needs of Refugee and Asylum Seeking Young People: A Review of the Literature*, published by Department for Education and Skills in 2005 and 'The role of education in the settlement of young refugees in the U.K: The Experiences of Young Refugees', in *Practice*, 17(3), (2005).

Maura Kearney is an experienced children and families practitioner, having worked in child protection, youth justice and asylum support. Her current practice focuses on private fostering. She is particularly interested in sharing practice learning and innovation with social work colleagues and other professionals who are working to safeguard children.

Selam Kidane was previously Refugee Children Consultant for British Association for Adoption and Fostering. Prior to that, she has worked for Family Service Units as a family therapist and doing outreach work on issues concerning refugees. She came to the United Kingdom seeking asylum as an unaccompanied child in the 1980s.

Ravi K. S. Kohli is Head of Applied Social Studies at the University of Bedfordshire. He migrated to the United Kingdom in 1969 with his family. He qualified as a social worker from York University in 1984. He has written *Social Work with Unaccompanied Asylum Seeking Children* published by Palgrave in 2007.

Fiona Mitchell is a Senior Researcher at The Children's Society. She previously worked at the University of York, where, together with Jim Wade and Graeme Baylis, she completed a study of social services responses to referrals of unaccompanied asylum seeking children. She is particularly interested in research and practice that promotes the participation of children and young people in decision making about their lives.

Hitesh Raval has worked as a clinical psychologist and systemic family psychotherapist primarily in Children and Adolescent Mental Health Services (CAMHS). He maintains his clinical interest in working with diversity and across languages within the therapeutic context. His research interests include child and family mental health, multicultural dimensions to mental health and therapeutic practice and therapeutic work involving language interpreters. He is currently working at Essex University as the Programme Director for the Professional Doctorate in Clinical Psychology.

Irene Sclare is a Consultant Clinical Psychologist, and lead psychologist for Child and Adolescent Mental Health Services (CAMHS) in South London and Maudsley NHS Trust. She is the lead for young refugee and asylum seeker mental health in Southwark CAMHS where she works directly with young refugees, as well as providing training and supervision to colleagues in other teams and agencies. She was coordinator of the Young Refugee Mental Health Project, which was based at the Maudsley Hospital for three years until October 2004.

John Simmonds is Director of Policy, Research and Development at the British Association for Adoption and Fostering. He has a wide interest in children who are separated from their birth parents and the policy, practice and research issues that arise from this. He co-edited *Direct Work with Children* with Jane Aldgate in 1988 and has published many articles over the past 25 years.

He recently had an article published in *Adoption and Fostering*, 28 (2) in Summer 2004 called 'Primitive forces in society: Holding the unaccompanied asylum seeking child in mind'.

Jim Wade is a Senior Research Fellow in the Social Work Research and Development Unit, University of York. His main research interests are in the area of social work and related services for vulnerable groups of children and young people, including looked after children, care leavers, young runaways and unaccompanied asylum seeking children. He has been involved in the preparation of best practice guides and official guidance on services for care leavers and young runaways and has acted as consultant to other national and international research initiatives in these areas.

Introduction

Ravi K. S. Kohli and Fiona Mitchell

This is a story a social worker told one of us during a research interview about her practice with an unaccompanied asylum seeking young person, of whom she was very fond. They had known each other for about three years, and he was on the cusp of moving towards independent living. She described him as fashion conscious, clean and tidy, and someone who was self-reliant and liked order. He had no close friends, and the social worker felt that he could use his charm to get what he wanted from people. He was said to like music and 'glamorous living'. He was learning to be a bricklayer, and was very enthusiastic about his training. He was seen as talented by his teachers – someone who had a good eye for a straight line and could build perfect walls. To calm himself, this young man would build and build. His social worker said that he would become angry and distressed sometimes, and even though she knew some of his history of great harm, it was not always clear to her what the triggers for his feelings were on a day-to-day basis. However, just as the social worker liked him, he liked the social worker. 'Oh, you're like my mum', he would say sometimes. The social worker was asked to think about the young person's network of belonging in later life, after he left the care of social services. She said, taking into account that his whole family had been destroyed in the country of origin, that he had said to her that 'in order to get a family, I'll have to make a family'. Then, he had said, he would build his family a house.

The social worker said that she had chosen to tell this story to us because it reminded her of the rebuilding that needed to happen for many of the unaccompanied young people she worked with, and that while it illustrated an individual's personal ground zero in a stark way, it also showed endurance as part of a broad pattern of challenges and possibilities facing young asylum seekers as they search for resettlement. This book contains many such stories about capability in the face of hardship that are emerging as part of contemporary responses to the welfare needs of unaccompanied asylum seeking children and young people – a capability that is shared between providers and users of a range of services in health and social care as the lives of unaccompanied minors are rebuilt over time in the United Kingdom. The contributors recognise that there are several major goals facing unaccompanied children arriving at any nation related to achieving safety and the legal right to remain, feeling connected to others, and becoming accomplished economically and educationally. They also recognise that the responses helpers need to make are complex, where each encounter with an unaccompanied minor raises questions and issues about 'us' and 'them' as the relationship between the child or young person and their helper evolves over time. It is this interplay between those of us who are established and powerful within our territories and those who are newly (and perhaps warily) moving into them, that we initially want to examine here.

Us and them: relating to unaccompanied minors

To be comforted by the folds of common citizenship is an experience that many of us take for granted. Our sense of who we are, our location and position within the territory that we inhabit, and our capacity to visit our history – either through our personal narrative or family membership and broader community ties – remains a foundation for a rhythmic life, where we can make sense of the patterns of moving backwards and forwards along the routes of belonging that connect us to other people. Within this sphere of existence, we are in charge, and can stand still and move as and when we choose. Visiting other places and coming home seem natural and unthwarted acts, because our lives are relatively safe. In being able to afford continuity, and in displaying the details of our natural selves within our day-to-day lives, we can experience ourselves as individuals, as well as members of communities that through luck and perseverance have achieved a level of stability and are relatively calm and still. Our world is ours, and we experience ourselves as ordinary people, enduring the rough and tumble of our lives without being blown away, because many pegs hold us in place, whether they are people, owned spaces, belongings or documents that confirm our entitlement to remain and prosper within our territories.

In contrast, if we consider the lives and circumstances of children and young people enduring forced migration, a very much more contingent picture emerges. We know through a variety of research studies that are discussed in this book, that becoming a refugee is something that happens to you – it is not an act of self-determination but a product of someone else's actions against you. Here, the pegs are uprooted, places abandoned and people and possessions lost in the process of departure from home towards another place, often unknown. Particularly in the shredding of civic obligations during times of civil war, the loss of ordinariness and the absence of rhythm and routine signal the transition from a complex and detailed life to one which is full of risk. Moreover, these events and actions lead to the creation of a compacted identity, where what is most visible is the label on the outside of a 'refugee' and an 'asylum seeker'. It is by the presentation and judgement of this outside packaging, that the terms of entry into host nations are negotiated. In a sense, children and young people who are forced migrants make the journey away from harm, yet at the same time the journey makes them (Turton, 1979), as they shift from a full and detailed life to a regulated, scrutinised and labelled existence, however extensive or short lived the transition. While these labels have an administrative utility, it is through their usage that individuality and ordinariness are compromised, and 'thick' lives reduced to 'thin' descriptions (Kohli, 2006).

We – that is citizens who have always had a choice about remaining where we are and holding on to our details of ordinary living – can see them as sketched-in people who do not have that choice. We can see them in outline form, described by their asylum status. In addition, the label can be read as a threat or a need (or indeed an assortment of shades between bad and sad) by observers, depending on their own perspectives. For example, in a paper discussing the concept of forced migration, Turton (2004) notes the tendency to see refugees as victims in many aspects of research into their lives. Moreover, he says that the language used in receiving nations to describe refugees is often constructed by people who are powerful and stable in their territory describing people who are relatively powerless and on the move. Here he suggests that when we talk about migrant trickles, flows, waves and floods the image that is constructed is of some kind of natural event (perhaps a disaster) that we did not bring about but now have a responsibility to deal with. Perhaps while refugees are represented in this way – as molecules in the liquid flow of particular forms of experience, they are at risk of being perceived as an undifferentiated mass, from people who are their helpers, as well as those who choose to build higher dams to keep themselves from being watered down. Given these risks – of seeing victims or charlatans, of categorising them from different, sometimes polarised perspectives, and of not seeing details – how can we begin to understand what it is really like to seek resettlement following forced migration in a way that allows people who are asylum seekers and refugees to be seen as 'ordinary people driven by ordinary desires, such as wanting to live in peace in a democracy that allows free speech' (Robinson and Segrott, 2002: 64).

In order to address this question, this book explores some key issues in reference to the lives of unaccompanied children seeking asylum. In theoretical terms the book broadly relies on a social constructionist approach to practice that allows several meanings of specific phenomena to co-exist. The process of facilitating resettlement, for example, is defined in three ways – first, as practical assistance in the social world; second as a way of therapeutic helping that allows distress to be managed; and third, as a way of providing long-term companionability and friendship for unaccompanied minors. Similarly, a simple approach to experiencing refugees as having 'tragic identities' is dissolved in favour of a fuller account that engages with their will to resettle and their 'survivability' in the face of danger and opportunity. Finally, stories from refugee children and their helpers are presented in ways that allow people to speak of their experiences 'in the round'. This fits firmly within constructive social work practice that pursues 'what is happening when the problem is not happening' (Parton and O'Byrne, 2000: 56), so that refugee children are seen as real people with real lives that are marked by peaks, troughs, optimism and a willingness to dwell in possibility.

Defining the use of terms and labels

A number of terms are used in the book to describe the group of children and young people whose lives are the focus of the discussion in the chapters. In general, three descriptors are used to define the group – one that defines their status as legal minors, one that describes their separation from their parents, customary care givers or legal guardian, and one that defines their immigration status as people who have entered the country seeking asylum. In this book, the different authors employ different terms to refer to the groups that they are discussing. Sometimes this is meaningful, but at other times the reader should accept the terms used as a short hand. Therefore, some pointers are provided here for the reader to bear in mind as they read the chapters.

References are made to 'children', 'young people' and 'minors'. In the main, authors are referring to people who are under the age of 18. Sometimes authors make a distinction between children and young people when they are drawing attention to variability in the needs of older or younger minors. Sometimes they are intending to refer to all under the age of 18 but use the terms child and young person interchangeably or use one or other of the terms for the sake of brevity. Where authors are referring to 'young people', who are over the age of 18, they make this clear by referring to them as young adults.

The term 'unaccompanied', in the context of asylum seeking and refugee children, is commonly used to denote a child or young person who arrived into the country of asylum without a parent or customary caregiver. There has been some effort on the part of international NGOs to emphasise that what is of import is the child's separation from the adults who traditionally or legally provide them with care and protection (Separated Children in Europe Programme, 2004). Indeed it is important to bear in mind that a child could be physically 'accompanied' by an adult or have some connection to an adult in a country of asylum but be without an adult who can provide care or protection. Such circumstances are encompassed within the use of the term 'unaccompanied' in this book, and fit with the guidelines offered by the United Nations High Commission for Refugees which states that unaccompanied children are 'those who are separated from both parents and are not being cared for by an adult who, by law or custom, is responsible to do so' (UNHCR, 1994: 121).

The authors of the chapters refer to refugee and asylum seeking children and young people who are unaccompanied. These terms include those who are seeking asylum, those who have been granted temporary leave to remain and those who have been recently granted refugee status. The reader should bear in mind that there are differences in the legal status and entitlements of these groups, and that these can have significant implications. For example, the granting of indefinite leave to remain, under the terms of the 1951 UN Convention on the Status of Refugees, brings with it legal status and entitlement that can ease the practical, social, economic and psychological uncertainties that individuals do face when seeking asylum. Sometimes authors are drawing the readers' attention to such differences and use the terms asylum seeker/ seeking and refugee to demarcate them. At other times, authors use the terms interchangeably to emphasise the similarities that exist for the different groups.

The topics discussed in the following chapters have relevance for the lives of all children and young people who are separated from their parents or customary care givers and entered the country to seek asylum, irrespective of their current immigration status.

Ways of understanding the experience of unaccompanied children

This book presents accounts from several areas of practice with unaccompanied asylum seeking and refugee minors. As these differing accounts are put together, the authors illuminate aspects of working with distress and uncertainty, as well as capability and resilience. They focus on resettlement as a political, legal and personal goal, as well as a process of healing and recovery over time. They describe how these children and young people recover a sense of lost ordinariness for themselves following fragmentation from their original homes. They also offer accounts of using tools, skills and resources in a judicious, clear and consistent manner. In doing so, the book offers ways of understanding the experience of refugee children that are built on recognising capability within the helpers, the recipients of help, and the contexts within which assistance is provided. Their experiences as displaced children and their specific needs as forced migrants are brought together within the belief that effective resettlement is possible, and that policies, laws, organisational strategies and practices can be threaded together in ways that allow the children and young people to recover and reach out towards futures that are less sharply fragmented than their past. Practitioners and policy makers are shown within the book as engaging in coherent acts of assistance.

The initial three chapters are such because they stimulate thought on how we can explore our own understandings of the 'predicament' of unaccompanied children, the helping relationship and the process of resettlement. In Chapter 1, Simmonds meditates on the power of narrative and appeals to us to reflect on the construction of stories and the meanings that we take from them. In Chapter 2, Dennis also appeals to the reader to continually re-evaluate our interpretations of the impact of legal and policy frameworks on social work practice. She presents an analysis of the legal and policy frameworks that govern social work with unaccompanied asylum seeking and refugee children, and considers how social work ethics and values can remain at the core of practice despite the apparent clashes, constraints and constrictions which result from the interaction between immigration and welfare legislation. In Chapter 3, Kohli explores a series of stories told by practitioners about their work with unaccompanied children and reflects on the differing meanings that are attributed by practitioners and by those who seek to understand or explain contemporary social work practice.

The following six chapters each focus upon an aspect of practice. Chapters 4 and 5 discuss aspects of assessment practice, with Mitchell writing on initial and ongoing needs assessment within a social work context and Raval on the inter-relationship between young people, bi-lingual co-workers and practitioners in the context of mental health assessment and treatment. Chapter 6 by Heaphy et al. also explores the building of therapeutic relationships but in the context of group work among unaccompanied young women. Chapters 7 and 8 consider the use of family placements, with Kearney describing her team's approach to facilitating the placement of unaccompanied children and young people and Hek reflecting on the value of foster placements for the care and resettlement of unaccompanied children. In Chapter 9, Dixon and Wade review transition planning and support in preparation for unaccompanied children reaching their eighteenth birthday and beyond.

In the final Chapter, Kidane draws on her own personal history and on that of others, who came to the United Kingdom as unaccompanied children seeking asylum to reflect on their experiences of growing up. The testimonies emphasise their feelings of pain, loss and despair as well as their resilience in the face of their ongoing search for a sense of belonging, connection and purpose in their lives.

The book proposes that unaccompanied asylum seeking children and young people are, by and large, capable people who can resettle in different ways if they are given opportunities and resources that maintain a sense of well-being and connectedness. In order to re-establish roots in the United Kingdom, the contributors assert that several different aspects of resettlement journeys need to be undertaken simultaneously, including the practical and emotional journeys leading to a coherent sense of the minors as people who can belong again to a new environment, within which loss and gain can be managed effectively. The conditions that can create or impede a smooth progression as described within this book focus on laws, policies, tools and skills. While the book attempts to illuminate a variety of ways that refugee and asylum seeking children and young people can be assisted towards resettlement, its purpose is not instructive. Instead some of the parameters of what are reliable strategies and practices are laid out, with an invitation for others to use them in meaningful ways dependent on their own contexts and frames of reference. What the contributors assert is that finding people who are trustworthy, finding opportunities to succeed in their social worlds, and finding laws, policies and protocols that shelter a sense of rootedness are key determinants of effective practice with unaccompanied minors. They are the catalytic converters, helping these children and young people to move from fragmentation to coherence over time.

References

Kohli, R. K. S. (2006). The sound of silence: listening to what unaccompanied children say and do not say, *British Journal of Social Work*, 36: 707–721.

Parton, N. and O'Byrne, P. (2000). *Constructive Social Work: Towards a New Practice*. Basingstoke: Palgrave Macmillan.

Robinson, V. and Segrott, J. (2002). *Understanding the Decision-Making of Asylum Seekers*, Finding 172. London: Home Office Research, Development and Statistics Directorate.

Separated Children in Europe Programme (2004). *Separated Children in Europe Programme: Statement of Good Practice*, 3rd edn. Geneva: International Save the Children Alliance in Europe, United Nations High Commission for Refugees.

Turton, D. (1979). A journey made them: territorial; segmentation and ethnic identity among the Mursi. In L. Holy (ed.), *Segmentary Lineage Systems Reconsidered. Queen's University Papers in Social Anthropology*, vol. 4. Belfast: Queen's University Press, pp. 119–143.

Turton, D. (2004). *The meaning of place in a world of movement: lessons from long-term field research in Southern Ethiopia*. RSC Working Paper 18. University of Oxford, International Development Centre.

United Nations High Commission for Refugees. (1994). *Refugee Children: Guidelines on Protection and Care*. Geneva: UNHCR.

CHAPTER 1

Telling the Stories of Unaccompanied Asylum Seeking and Refugee Children

John Simmonds

> It might be difficult for some people to understand about refugee children. If they want to stay happy then they do not want to hear our story.
>
> Abdoul, a young man from Somalia (quoted in Kidane, 2001: 38)

Introduction

Social work with unaccompanied refugee children presents social workers with a new challenge. The position of children so completely dislocated from their parents, family, country, culture, language and religion is not replicated in the issues facing professionals working with UK children. Added to this is the traumatic experiences of many children who have faced war, civil conflict or persecution. And lastly there is the unresolved issue of their status as asylum seekers. This makes them an extremely vulnerable group. However, within this there is much evidence of enormous resilience, strength and determination. Finding a way of relating to this very challenging issue means understanding some very complex stories. These stories have many dimensions to them – political, social, psychological and historical. Bringing this together in a chapter which reflects this complexity has meant identifying some helpful concepts and then exploring them in a way that illustrates not only how they might be used but most particularly how they might develop over time. I have chosen to do this by re-telling the story of Andersen's 'The Ugly Duckling'. The reader is then invited to use their imagination to make connections between the concepts outlined at the beginning of the chapter, the words of unaccompanied children themselves and a fairy tale.

Stories and their meanings

Stories about unaccompanied asylum seeking children and young people often tell us about victims, villains and those who try to help, roles that exist in an intimate triangular relationship with each other. They are often very complex stories that span thousands of miles, mountains, plains and rivers; of courage, chance encounters, kindly gestures, heroic struggles, pain and sometimes even death. They are stories that need to be told, they need to be listened to with a curiosity about their meaning and context (Cecchin, 1987) and with respect. But they are stories that can easily be distorted because they become part of the narratives told by others – narratives that emphasise the securing of a country's borders or the fear of strangers, unknown lands, strange tongues and customs. The child's story then comes to have meaning not just for itself but because of the part that it plays in the greater narrative of the state. For instance, an unaccompanied child's age no longer tells us when they were born and when to celebrate their birthday but whether they can stay in the United Kingdom, what and how much they should get of the state's resources and whether they might be sent back to where they come from. Whether the story of their age should be told at all or told truthfully becomes an issue of great significance because of the implications that it may have for decisions about the child. However, too fierce and quick a pursuit of truth about a young person's age can become a dangerous thing and can easily be the making of both a villain and a victim when it is a part of the state's story telling for keeping children out.

> When I arrived we were asked by the Tigrinia translator how old we were. I could not remember the word for eight and by mistake I said I was nine. (Rahwa, an 8-year old Eritrean girl (Kidane, 2001: 16))

Social work and stories

Story telling in either oral or written form is a deeply embedded part of human culture and most people become adept at doing so from an early age. Social work has a primary interest in people, their relationships, circumstances, histories, tragedies, loves and losses. To be a good social worker, you have to be able to tell a good story and that story will inevitably include you as one of the characters. If you don't have an interest in stories, then you probably won't find social work very interesting or rewarding. If you don't feel comfortable at becoming a character in other people's stories, then this may come to dominate how you go about doing social work – anxious, avoidant and disconnected. Having said this, social work is not commonly thought of as a story making or a story telling activity. If anything it has attempted to distance itself from such a description by wrapping itself in the cloak of science – its evidence base, technology – needs assessments, care planning, purchaser/provider split, or bureaucracy – political, regulatory or resource accountability. All of these are stories in themselves – albeit cast in a particular narrative mould. They may need to be listened to and may well have important things to tell us but it is important not to confuse these stories with the stories that those people who come into contact with social workers as service users or clients might tell. Their stories will almost certainly focus on a narrative, which talks of respect, love, belonging, being listened to; of grief, tragedy, loss and despair. When social workers come into contact with these stories, it is essential that they treat them with respect. While it may be important to be curious about these stories in order to understand them, this curiosity must proceed with care. Human beings are remarkably resistant to their stories being re-interpreted or re-told by others particularly when they are people with power. Stories are precious to people because they define who they are, where they come from and what they are connected to. Re-telling them needs to be done with considerable care if they are not to be experienced as nonsense, a lie or an assault. Social workers need to be expert at listening to stories and expert at being storytellers.

All this poses something of a challenge because the state and its systems impose their own ways of story telling – scientific, technological and bureaucratic. For example, enormous energy has gone into the subsequent telling of the story of Victoria Climbie's appalling death at the hands of her aunt and new boyfriend after they arrived from West Africa to make a better life for themselves. However, while it was her carers that killed her when they were meant to care for her, most people will remember a story of failed bureaucracy – of the lack of social work, health and police action despite numerous opportunities to do so. This resulted in one of the most significant public inquiries for a decade (Laming, 2003). It was a tragedy of epic proportions, with an innocent victim, numerous villains and no happy ending. Nobody wanted to know or could bear to hear the unfolding story of Victoria or her Aunt from the point at which they arrived in the United Kingdom or their journey together eventually to be joined by a boyfriend who tortured and then killed Victoria. While many people got to know of them as characters during this journey, they existed as disconnected and superficial elements in the story that health and social services told because the connecting narrative was wrongly reported or hidden and largely unknown. Nobody could see or tell the unfolding story before them because it was something that existed only in transitory fragments in different professionals' minds. It was therefore a story without meaning, impact or consequent action. There was an absence of curiosity but unlike the cat, it was this absence that resulted in a killing.

The way the story was eventually, formally, told by Lord Laming has itself generated another energetic story with new primary legislation, a wholesale shake up of the system for delivering children's services and the introduction of a vast computer system for tracking every child in England. What it has also done is to give a stern community warning to professionals, as good stories should do, 'Do not become a part of a similar story as villainy beckons you.'

But if curiosity is the key to the prevention of a killing or indeed the resolution of other human issues, then professionals must become engaged and involved if they are to understand the story, tell it in a helpful way and maybe even do something helpful to change it. After all, computers don't tell good stories. But the problem with becoming involved in these kind of stories is the threat of then being seen as a professional villain if something goes wrong with all that can be meted out to them. Listening to and telling the story of others in vulnerable situations needs to be carefully handled. Professionals in such positions are very exposed. They need to be able to tell their own stories, about what they have seen or done, to somebody who will listen also with curiosity and respect – in supervision, to colleagues or consultants.

The power of stories

Telling and being told a story is something that is a part of every child's experience. Stories can be exciting, upsetting, scary and moving. They have a beginning, a middle and usually a happy ending. Stories rely on facts but their meaning is in the imagination they conjure up and the emotions they evoke. Stories work by involving children with characters in the story that they can identify with – heroes and heroines, witches and villains, animals, relationships, love, worries, triumphs and even disasters. The child's identification with these characters is something that happens on the insides of children – in their minds – although the story describes events that are discernibly on the outside – on the page, in the film, on the stage or more likely on television. If the distinction between what is in the imagination of the child and what exists in reality seriously breaks down, the child may be having a nightmare or developing a psychotic illness. The problems children have in managing this distinction can be seen in Hodges and Steele (2000); (Hodges et al., 2003) in the development and use of story stem narrative techniques to assess their emotional development. In these, children who have been seriously maltreated can be made so anxious when asked to complete a short story involving an imagined child or animal, that they can have great difficulty in engaging with the story, beginning to think how it might end or when they do, invent violent and bizarre endings.

While stories are constructed in imagination, they work because they represent an important truth about reality although this may be in an exaggerated or a one-dimensional way. If the story does not link to something that has the ring of truth about it for the listener or reader, then the story serves little purpose or interest. The development of a child's capacity to construct and to understand stories is complex. It relies heavily on the concept of 'mind mindedness' (Fonagy et al., 2002; Howe et al., 1999; Howe, 2005) – that other people have minds that work in particular ways and influences the way that they feel, think and behave. Understanding this is directly related to the way that the child's own mind has developed based on early intimate experiences of rhythmic synchronicity with primary caretakers. When this works well, feeling, thinking and behaviour become integrated into a coherent image of both the self and others. The development of this coherent sense of self is the basis for predicting how other people might respond to the individual's needs and also determines how they might respond. If a child has a predictive expectation of a warm and friendly response from other people expressed as a warm and friendly approach towards them, this is more likely to produce a warm and friendly response. This then has the potential to become a self-reinforcing cycle of positive emotion, thought and behaviour experienced in that relationship. However, a predictive expectation of a hostile or angry response from other children coded into a child's unfriendly or hostile behaviour towards another child might well produce an unfriendly, anxious or even hostile response. Developing the capacity to anticipate the world of relationships in the mind in a realistic and helpful way is crucial to being able to form cooperative, meaningful and satisfying relationships. But equally, fearful anticipation heightens the risk of a fearful response and can be a significant risk factor for the child and the cause of much misunderstanding and unhappiness. The development of a working and workable model (Bowlby, 1973) of relationships is core both to the development of self and the capacity to relate well to others (Winnicott, 1971).

These are complex child development and human relationship issues. But given they are so fundamental, the means by which ordinary people in ordinary circumstances develop and express them cannot be so complex. They must have a routine, everyday, comprehensible presence in the lives of people going about their business. This is why story making and story telling is so important. Stories convey the way that relationships are structured and the underlying meaning that these relationships have for the people involved in them. Whether these stories are spoken – the gossip in the street, over the dinner table, at work, over coffee or played out through 'soaps' or drama or printed in airport novels or more weighty literature, they are important because they continually present back to people a picture of the way the world works.

Karpman (1968) has identified a basic structure for understanding three critical roles that are present in and drive most stories. There are three principal roles – the role of victim, persecutor and rescuer. Each of these has their own dynamic. First, there is the overt role – the way that the character typically behaves towards other characters in the story and second, its function as a defence against feelings which are experienced as unbearable. For example, when a character takes the role of 'victim' in a story, it acts as a defence against that character's own aggression or hostility; the role of persecutor is a defence against vulnerability and distress; and the role of rescuer is a defence against the individual's vulnerability and aggression. The character's role and the associated defence are complimentary to each other. While therefore the role might have painful consequences as 'lived experience', for example, being a victim, it is necessary for the character to stay in that role because the feelings being defended against are feared to be more painful and/or unbearable. For each character there is an internal splitting into the role that is lived out as the story unfolds and the denied feelings. The defence operates by splitting off the unbearable feelings and projecting them into a character whose role then directly expresses these feelings. For the victim, aggressive or hostile feelings are defended against by being split off and projected into an individual whose necessary defence against vulnerability puts them in the role of persecutor. For the persecutor, feelings of vulnerability are split off and projected into the victim. And for the rescuer both sets of unbearable feelings are respectively split off into the victim and the persecutor (Liotti, 1999).

While then the three roles are distinct and identifiable with characters in the story, the process of defensive splitting creates powerful complimentary relationships – that of persecutor–victim; rescuer–victim; rescuer–persecutor. Each role is interlocked with another role and cannot exist without it. When these roles become characters in stories, the impetus of the narrative sets out how the victim becomes victimised by the persecutor and eventually rescued by the rescuer to produce what is usually a happy ending. However, in order to make stories interesting, the characters' roles may change. as the narrative develops. Persecutors may become victims and victims, persecutors. Although the underlying structure of these roles and their relationships may be quite simple, the art of the story teller is in weaving a narrative around these roles that is rich, dramatic, entertaining and identifiable.

These two different components of mind mindedness and the drama triangle need to be brought together. Relationships can be thought of as having two different components to them, the cooperative, reciprocal, needs meeting, problem solving component (Heard et al., 1997) built on the general expectation that the 'other' (person) is attentive, open, responsive and engaged. The other component is defensive. Individuals need to defend themselves, especially when they are emotionally vulnerable, from encounters with 'other' people where openness, responsiveness and engagement are not present or cannot be relied upon. While these defences are emotional/cognitive in operation, they are structured in relationships on the basis of how one person experiences the other. I have suggested elsewhere (Simmonds 1998; 2000) that the development of a working and workable awareness of the three roles described by Karpman and their accompanying narrative in the mind of a child becomes a map of the way defences are constructed in relationships. This builds on the contribution of attachment theory as the most highly articulate view of the importance of internal models of experience in relationships as the basis for the capacity to relate to others in the emotional and social world.

Take, for instance, a secure attachment script – 'If I need comfort because I am distressed after a brief separation, then the person (attachment figure) I turn to will respond directly and in an appropriately comforting way (happy ending).' There is much that the child can positively infer from this narrative sequence, especially when it is numerously repeated, about their self-worth, what they can expect from significant others and how they can find comfort if they need it. As a story, it is reassuring but its interest is probably elsewhere, as it should be, because as a narrative sequence, it releases the child from whatever anxiety and discomfort they are experiencing to explore and find out about the world 'out there'. However, where individuals have attachment scripts that are continuously activated, they are compromised in their capacity to helpfully explore the external world as the following script highlights. 'If I need comfort because I am distressed, then the person (attachment figure) I turn to responds in a way that leaves me feeling confused, distressed or frightened (a victim persecuted by their attachment figure). Maybe somebody else will comfort me (rescuer).' There is much that a child might infer from this narrative sequence. Is it because of who I am that the person I have turned to has responded in a way that has left me feeling distressed/frightened? If I am a person with bad feelings, then I must be a bad person. I will not let anyone else see my distress or maybe it is better not to get distressed in the first place or look for any comfort. As a narrative sequence this has the potential to create a victim in children who are powerfully locked into a persecuting relationship with their attachment figure. They cannot satisfactorily turn away from their attachment figure to explore the outside world because of the uncertainty about their availability.

The story of the ugly duckling

Many children and adults will be familiar with Hans Christian Andersen's story of the 'Ugly Duckling' although this may only be with the tidied up, modern version. In its original version it is a powerful and haunting tale of great psychological and social complexity and intensity. What is remarkable about it is the fact that the story is told in just a few pages and is therefore highly condensed. Although the story has a relatively straightforward narrative to it, the relationships and their context can be understood as symbolic representations of a much deeper and universal reality. The opening paragraph sets a scene of rustic tranquillity, with a mother duck waiting and watching for her nest of eggs to hatch. There is a description and awareness of a wider world beyond the nest but the river's edge is the place where the baby ducks can and will belong. However, two facts disturb this apparent tranquillity. The first is the absence of the mother's partner – 'the wretch, he never comes to visit me!' But this part of the story is never told – we don't know if his absence results from irresponsibility in caring for his pregnant partner or maybe from matters outside his control – is he imprisoned for political activity or maybe he is fighting in the army. The second issue is the presence of the one egg that won't hatch. An older duck gives a dire warning about the likely identity of this egg given its size and appearance and suggests it may be a turkey. Family and community cohesion seem to be threatened by its presence and the mother duck is advised to abandon her care of the egg. She resists this but when it does hatch she is horrified 'How big and ugly he was!' and she tests his identity as a duck by forcing him into the water – sink (death) or swim (survive). He swims and survives and despite his size and his ugly appearance, she identifies him as one of her own and develops a real pride in him.

> Look how beautifully he uses his legs and how straight he holds himself! He's my own child and make no mistake! He's really handsome if you look at him properly! (216)

Having claimed him as her child, she wants to show him off in her community. She takes her responsibility as a mother seriously. She teaches all her children to show respect for the status of other community members and particularly to be deferential in their behaviour to the elders in the farmyard. It is an important lesson for the ducklings as new community members. But we also come to see that this is also a community under threat. Food is scarce and fights take place and the presence of this new family as competitors for scarce resources produces a violent reaction from existing community members. And as the individual that stands out, it is the ugly duckling that is seen as the source of the threat and receives the brunt of hostile community feeling and over time 'it grew worse and worse'.

> The poor duckling was chased about by everyone; even his brothers and sisters were unkind to him, and kept on saying, If only the cat would get you, you ugly thing!' ... The ducks bit him, and the hens pecked him, and the girl that fed the poultry kicked him with her foot. Then he ran off and flew away over the hedge. ... He came to the great marsh where the wild ducks lived. There he lay the whole night, he was so tired and unhappy. ... all he wanted was leave to lie in the rushes and drink a little of the marsh water. (218)

Now while this is not written as a story of an unaccompanied asylum seeking child, it has much of the perplexing anxiety and uncertainty of trying to make sense of who this newly arrived child is, 'so tired and unhappy' when they arrive at the great marsh of Heathrow or Dover. Where do they come from? Why are they here? What did they do? Who sent them? Is it their fault? Where are the parents? Are they a victim? Should we attack them? Let's send them back!

> It is not easy when people ask you lots of questions all the time – the Home Office, social workers, teachers, doctors – they all want to know why you are here. And sometimes it is difficult to tell everything. (Saadia – 15-year old girl from Somalia (Kidane, 2001: 38))

And what is the child to make of this terrifying experience – is this just a story or is it for real? Have I imagined this? What did I do? Is this a nightmare, am I going mad? The children's perspective on what has happened to them will determine how they explain and understand their story. It may also determine their capacity to survive these events. A child that explains difficult events or experiences as 'That's because I'm so ugly!' is not in a strong position to develop a helpful internal dialogue that mediates the emotional and practical challenge of life. Whether these events are the emotional roller coaster of family or peer relationships, the challenge of school, physical development or the asylum process, children and young people need to be able to draw on both those resources they have inside of them and what exists in the world around them. These need to be seen and experienced in a helpful and supportive way.

There are also untold stories in Andersen's tale as there often are with unaccompanied children – what did the ugly duckling's mother make of the disappearance of her child – was she relieved, was she grieving for him, had she noticed at all with all the mouths she had to feed? And the siblings – what had they noticed, did they care, might he come back? This quotation from a 12-year old poignantly describes this.

> My head is filled with worrying about my parents, my sister and my brother who is not eating that well and he cries in his sleep. We have been in London for a week and I still find it difficult to not think about you all. What time would it be there now? What might be happening at school? Which teacher will be teaching? It is as if my heart is still there. (Letter to a friend in Eritrea from a 12-year old but never sent because there was no known address to send it to – Kidane, 2001: 17)

Both policy and practice in relation to unaccompanied children take a strong interest in these stories and what they mean. Immigration and social services can impose stories of their own – political and bureaucratic – scripts dominated by concerns about border control, asylum determination and then by the statutory framework to assess and plan for a child's care. But the official story is not the only story – there might need to be accounts of political and community unrest and conflict, of mothers that defend and educate their children as best they know how, of mothers who struggle with their own survival and see their children snatched from them or disappear. Or the story of the journey itself.

Taking a journey is something that most people do – it may be for work, it may be for a holiday, it may be temporary or it may be for good. Like a story, journeys can be exciting, upsetting, frightening and moving. We might try to minimise a sense of being unsettled by using a reputable travel agent, being specific about when we want to leave and arrive and where we want to go, how we want to travel and where we want to stay and eat and what we want to do. But taking control in this way is not a guarantee that things will work out as expected or that we will not be disappointed or upset. There are risks in taking journeys.

For unaccompanied children, the journey they take from their homeland can be understood as a personal journey but it is also a family, community and a political journey. But as a journey, it may share little with the process described above because it is marked by the overwhelming feature of fleeing from a place (called home) that is intolerable, by way of a journey that is also intolerable, to something that is unknown (asylum). The ugly duckling's journey is neither planned nor safe. It is a desperate response to dangerous and intolerable attacks from within the community where his instinctive need to survive and to protect himself is overwhelming. The risks in the journey quickly becomes apparent as he is befriended by two geese who point to another marsh where 'some lovely sweet wild geese, young ladies every one of them' live. They advise him to 'try your luck with them!' But as is the case with fellow travellers or traffickers all is not quite as reassuring as it seems for 'Bang! Bang! ... both the wild ganders fell down dead and the water became red with blood.' A shoot was in progress and the sound of war continued to echo around the marsh filling the ugly duckling with more terror, especially as a 'frightful great dog ... thrust his muzzle right down towards the duckling and bared his sharp teeth' ... but then disappears without touching him. Even this lucky escape is interpreted by the ugly duckling in his own way 'I'm so ugly that even the dog will think twice before it bites me!'

The desperate journey continues until the ugly duckling is taken in by an old woman, her cat and a hen. This becomes a short-term foster placement where the old woman offers a three-week trial on the understanding that the ugly duckling will produce duck eggs. It is a strange reversal of what the duckling needs – somebody who understands and can relate to him and his story. Instead, he finds no place in this family. They are too preoccupied with their own values of 'cleverness' to care for the duckling's need to swim and dive. Kidane's (2001) collection of refugee children's voices and experiences echoes the duckling's sense of displacement, and confirms that finding a place of your own, in a new country, in a new culture, with a new family when its members are preoccupied with stories of their own to defend, is a very difficult thing to do. If finding a place is to happen, then it needs to be driven by a combination of respect, curiosity and engagement on the part of those that are the host. But it means opening hearts and minds to loss, distress and the inevitable vulnerability that comes from this. When the duckling can stand the foster home no longer, his 'going out into the wide world' is not an act of independence or rebellion but an act of despair. It continues to put the duckling in the role of victim and powerfully creates an image of a persecutory old woman, her cat and the hen. In the nature of a defensive script, it resolves nothing and perpetuates danger for the duckling. There is, however, some glimmer of hope when the duckling catches sight of a flock of swans 'shining white with long graceful necks ... they spread their splendid great wings and flew away from those cold parts to warmer lands and open lakes' (224).

There is a hint of rescue here with the duckling being instinctively drawn towards his own ethnic group but after losing sight of them and diving to the bottom of the lake, he surfaces in an agitated state,

> He did not know what the birds were called nor where they where flying to, and yet he felt more deeply drawn towards them than he had ever been to anything. (224)

This is a powerful emergence of an attachment script, a mother lost, glimpsed in the distance and stirring up deep, powerful memories and feelings of longing and identification. But his mother knows nothing of this. The duckling reminds himself that he is the cause of this great tragedy 'poor, ugly creature that he was!' and is immersed in a bleak, freezing emotional and social landscape 'he was tired out; he lay quite still and froze fast in the ice'. The brief glimpse and memory of a past relationship where his mother was proud and caring ices over.

But he is rescued from this terrible episode in his journey by a farm labourer who breaks the ice and takes him home where he recovers (Harris et al., 2001). On the surface this is a more friendly foster family full of lively, playful children, warm milk and tubs of butter. But the duckling has become traumatised and fearful and the children's playful approach to him is experienced as an attack and in a panic, he flies into the butter and then the flour. His foster mother strikes out at him to defend her home, her children fall over one another to catch him and in a desperate attempt to defend himself, he flies out of the door 'into the bushes and the new fallen snow – and there he lay as if in a swoon'.

What therefore starts out as a rescuer foster family ends up with a powerful description of the duckling being persecuted by them. But equally, the duckling is experienced as the persecutor of the family and their belongings as he misinterprets their inquisitive and lively interest in him as an attack. The defensive dynamic is played out again with a quick switching of roles. The vulnerability and traumatised position of the duckling is not understood and this becomes another experience where he is rejected and abandoned. Without the presence of a parent figure that can take up the role of reflective, respectful and curious adult, the duckling is locked into an endlessly repeating traumatising script. But then memories stir of what he once had –

> And right in front of him, out of the thick hanging branches, came three lovely white swans, ruffling their feathers and floating lightly on the water. The duckling recognised the magnificent birds and a strange sadness came over him. (226)

These become dangerous memories powerfully associated with his own sense of 'ugliness' and expectations of rejection and abandonment. He is both author of the script and victim to it. While his first response to the sight of the swans is to be mesmerised by them, his sadness is overwhelming and this is quickly followed by a wish for death. 'I will fly over to those kingly birds and they will peck me to death for daring to come near them. I'm so ugly.' At this point, he remembers all the rejections, abuse and trauma and decides that death is to be preferred. He flies towards the three swans who, seeing him rush at him.

> Only kill me! said the poor creature, bowing his head towards the water and awaiting his death.

The tragic consequences of this journey have finally come to a point of searing tension. The victim presents himself for sacrifice, the full weight of his life experiences having destroyed his will to communicate, to reach out, to be loved and to live. But in bowing his head towards the water he experiences something that quickly transforms the sense of who he is and what he might expect. The defensive and destructive power of the drama triangle evaporates and what is reflected back to him is a picture not of narcissistic but transformative love – 'he was no longer a dark grey bird, ugly and repulsive – he was himself a swan'. But this is no magic resolution because what has happened has come through the natural growth that results from a reflection back to the duckling of who he actually is – not a duckling but a maturing swan. He is seen for who he actually is and whatever perceived ugliness there might have been, in the eyes of a curious and respectful adult swan, this is transformed into something of beauty that is real and against which there does not need to be a defence.

'The Ugly Duckling' is a powerful psychological, political and social story. It is a story of a long and arduous journey by one individual at great risk compelled to search for a better life. In the process, he discovers who he is and the hatred he has developed for himself from life experiences and the responses of others becomes transformed into something of real beauty. The psychological process is both internal to the duckling – something he comes to see in himself and external – something that is reflected back to him by others. But it must be emphasised, this is not brought about by the avoidance of pain or the ugliness he sees or experiences. Andersen does require that we see and remember this as the story unfolds.

What is powerful about the story is the way Andersen gives an account of the intricate and complex emotional and cognitive processes underlying human development but through a story that has had immediate appeal to hundreds of thousands of children. It is a simple tale with an enduring moral message but its deeper meaning must move us beyond the pull of seeing the duckling as victim, the rest of the world as persecutors and the potential for social workers to become rescuers. This resolves nothing because these scripts are defensive traps, perpetuate themselves endlessly and do not stimulate growth. The whole story needs to be told, not just those parts of it, particularly the end, that create a sense of relief that the pain is over and the duckling has been saved.

Conclusion

The challenge for those working with unaccompanied asylum seeking children is in trying to see the whole story. It can be very appealing to see that work as the parallel of the ugly duckling story. What could be more enticing or rewarding than to be one of the three swans rushing over to rescue the duckling and convince him that he is also a swan. There are many barriers that make this difficult – the persecuting Home Office, the resource strapped local authority, the exploiting and dangerous traffickers or even the children or young persons themselves. But being identified with the role of rescuer is not helpful. We know from the story itself, that a primary identification as a rescuer (as with the farm labourer) does not prevent, the child experiencing us as a persecutor or indeed that we may experience ourselves as victims – of lies about age or the whereabouts of family or country of origin. Distancing ourselves from the triangle will not help either as the distance is likely to be experienced as persecuting.

If we become involved, we will need to understand the background and parallel stories that are integral to the unfolding narrative. First, we need to understand the story of what is happening inside the children, who they are, what makes them into the person they experience themselves as being. Second, we need to understand the story of what is happening between the children and those others that they are in a relationship with. And lastly we need to understand the influence of those group and inter-group factors that come from the social and political world. While each of these factors is a story in its own right, each influences the other in important ways. The ethnic tensions in the farmyard have a history behind them and can become the basis for hatred, violence and war. The pressure on the duckling's mum to reject him have a history. The outbreak of sibling rivalry has a history. They all come together in an outbreak of persecution and violence which is experienced as personal, but is generated by the political and the social world. In the end, this is what causes him to flee. None of this can be said to be his responsibility as it is described. The duckling is caught up in something that is not of his making particularly as a young child. But in his own mind it creates an ugliness that seriously interferes with his development. As the traumatic journey develops, it also influences his behaviour. The story then is of something that starts out on the outside of the duckling but ends up on the inside of him. But in his own experience this distinction is irrelevant because right up to the eventual resolution, the nightmare has become who he is.

Social workers inevitably become caught up in the swirling tensions of these issues – the political, the social, the inter personal and the personal. However, their capacity to actually influence most of them is negligible but this does not make them victims. But even if their relative lack of power is real, their position allows them to stand as observers to these events and their responsibility to the children and young people is to understand and tell these stories. But they need to be told by facing the 'ugliness' of fleeing and the conditions that bring it about. These need to be thought about and put into words. If young people's stories only exist as fragmentary, disconnected elements, they will have little impact and can become very dangerous. Re-telling them as bureaucratic, technological or scientific stories needs to proceed with great care and must not to be confused with the child's own story. In the end, what releases children and young people to grow and experience themselves as valued people who belong, feel love and can love is not the avoidance of ugliness – pain, loss

and despair but facing it. Children need contact with people whose minds are
open to this and are not afraid. At that point their experiences can be transformed and they can grow to become someone of real beauty.

References

Adcock, M. and White, R. (1998). *Significant Harm: Its Management and Outcome.*
  Croydon: Significant Publications.
Andersen, H. C. (1984). 'The Ugly Duckling'. In *Hans Andersens's Fairy Tales, A
  Selection*. Oxford: Oxford University Press.
Bowlby, J. (1973). *Attachment and Loss: Separation, Anxiety and Anger*. London: The
  Hogarth Press and Institute for Psychoanalysis.
Cecchin, G. (1987). Hypothesizing – Circularity – Neutrality revisited: an invitation to
  curiosity, *Family Process*, 26: 405–413.
Fonagy, P., Gergely, G., Jurist, E. and Target, M. (2002). *Affect Regulation,
  Mentalization and the Development of the Self*. New York: Other Press.
Harris, M. J. and Oppenheimer, D. (2001). *Into the Arms of Strangers: Stories of the
  Kindertransport*. London: Bloomsbury.
Heard, D. and Lake, B. (1997). *The Challenge of Attachment for Caregiving*. London:
  Routledge.
Hodges, J. and Steele, M. (2000). Effects of abuse on attachment representations;
  Narrative assessments of abused children, *Journal of Child Psychotherapy*, 26 (3):
  433–455.
Hodges, J., Steele, M., Hillman, S., Henderson, K. and Kaniuk, J. (2003). Changes in
  the attachment representations over the first year of adoptive placement: narratives
  of maltreated children, *Clinical Child Psychology and Psychiatry*, 8 (3): 351–367.
Howe, D. (2005). *Child Abuse and Neglect: Attachment, Development and
  Intervention*. Basingstoke: Palgrave Macmillan.
Howe, D., Brandon, M., Hinings, D. and Schofield, G. (1999). *Attachment Theory,
  Child Maltreatment and Family Support: A Practice and Assessment Model*.
  Basingstoke: Palgrave Macmillan.
Karpman, S. (1968). Fairy tales and script drama analysis, *Transactional Analysis
  Bulletin*, 7: 39–43.
Katz, I. and Treacher, A. (2000). *The Dynamics of Adoption: Social and Personal
  Perspectives*. London: Jessica Kingsley.
Kidane, S. (2001). *I Did Not Choose to Come Here- Listening to Refugee Children.*
  London: BAAF.
Laming, H. (2003). *The Victoria Climbie Inquiry: Report of an Inquiry by Lord
  Laming*. London: HMSO.
Liotti, G. (1999). Disorganisation of attachment as a model for understanding dis-
  sociative psychopathology. In J. Soloman and C. George (1999). *Attachment
  Disorganization*. New York and London: Guildford Press.
Simmonds, J. (1998). Making decisions in social work – persecuting, rescuing or being
  a victim. In M. Adcock and R. White (1998). *Significant Harm: Its Management
  and Outcome*. Croydon: Significant Publications.

——. (2000). The Adoption Narrative: Stories that we tell and those that we can't. In I. Katz and A. Treacher (2000). *The Dynamics of Adoption: Social and Personal Perspectives.* London: Jessica Kingsle.

Soloman, J. and George, C. (1999). *Attachment Disorganization.* New York and London: Guildford Press.

Winnicott, D. W. (1971). *Playing and Reality.* New York: Basic Books.

CHAPTER 2

The Legal and Policy Frameworks that Govern Social Work with Unaccompanied Asylum Seeking and Refugee Children in England

Judith Dennis

Introduction

In recent years, social work practitioners have become more experienced in their work with unaccompanied children, resulting in their increased awareness of the limitations placed on their work by the particular circumstances of the client group. It is often perceived by social work practitioners that immigration legislation 'overrides' the aims and objectives of social work itself. This incompatibility is sometimes expressed as a 'clash' or 'tension' between immigration policy and policy affecting children, including children who are in need of social work intervention. Guidance issued by the Association for Directors of Social Services (ADSS) makes recognition of this: 'Many social workers experience a tension between care and immigration legislation' (ADSS, 2005: 6).

This chapter aims to explore to what extent this is the case, through an analysis of the guiding principles and legal and policy frameworks within which social work with unaccompanied children seeking asylum is situated. The chapter will focus on the provision of a social work service by local authorities under the Children Act 1989 (herein described as 'the 1989 Act'). Whilst it may be of relevance, it will not explore the limitations placed on social services duties towards children considered to be 'accompanied' – who, since 2000, have not been eligible for services under the 1989 Act if their need is solely for alleviating destitution (see The Children's Legal Centre, 2003 for discussion on this).

Guiding principles of social work with children

In 2001, the International Federation of Social Workers and the International Association of Schools of Social Work issued the following definition of social work:

> The social work profession promotes social change, problem solving in human relationships and the empowerment and liberation of people to enhance wellbeing. Utilising theories of human behaviour and social systems, social work intervenes at the point where people interact with their environments. Principles of human rights and social justice are fundamental to social work. (BASW, 2002: 1)

The UK government's cross-departmental policy for children states on its Every Child Matters website that 'Social services play a central role in trying to improve outcomes for the most vulnerable and a key measure of success will be achieving change through closing the gap between their outcomes and those of the majority of children and young people.' We might, therefore, conclude that social justice is at the core of the social worker's function. In other words, social work is performed in order that change for the better may be realised.

Legislation and national policy governing social work with children

This principle of intervention to improve the outcomes for the target group is embodied in both legislation and policy. The 1989 Act imposes duties on local authorities to 'safeguard and promote the welfare of children within their area who are in need' (s.17 (1) (a)). An important principle of seeking and considering the child's wishes is highlighted in the same Act, introducing an additional duty to ensure that children have a say in what happens to them, for example, if the local authority is to become responsible for their care or 'accommodation' (s20 (6)). Unaccompanied children seeking asylum are not specifically mentioned in the 1989 Act itself, or in related guidance issued at the time. Later guidance, produced or endorsed by government, states or implies that they should be considered children in need. In 1995, the Department of Health asserted that 'these children are by definition living away from their parents: they are children in need' (1). In 2001, in a guide produced by the British Association for Adoption and Fostering (BAAF), and endorsed by the Department of Health, the definition of these children was once again placed firmly within the context of the 1989 Act 'Unaccompanied asylum seeking and refugee children have the same essential needs as all other children. As with other children in need, local authorities have the responsibility to ensure the safety and protection of refugee children as well as the promotion of their welfare' (Kidane, 2001: 3).

In addition to clarifying the responsibility of social work services towards unaccompanied children seeking asylum, government guidance has offered specific instruction as to the care and attention that should be paid to their circumstances and given clear direction as to how social workers should respond to them.

In 2000, the *Framework for Assessment of Children in Need and their Families* made it clear that not only should they be the focus of comprehensive needs assessments but it highlighted the sensitivity of their particular situation in a section entitled 'Assessment of Children in Special Circumstances'. This section (3.58) acknowledges that some children 'because of the nature of their problems or circumstances, will require particular care and attention during assessment. These are children ... whose wellbeing or need for immediate services may be overlooked and for whom subsequent planning and intervention may be less than satisfactory' (Department of Health, Education and Employment, Home Office, 2000: 47).

Unaccompanied children seeking asylum are described in the same section as those who 'without the care and protection of their parents or legal guardian ... having experienced or witnessed traumatic events ... may be suffering the most extreme forms of loss' (48). It is therefore widely accepted that unaccompanied children seeking asylum are to be provided with social work services by local authorities with guidance consistently drawing attention to their vulnerability.

Section 17 or Section 20?

Despite the legislative and policy framework just outlined, during the late 1990s it became common practice to provide a social work service to older unaccompanied children seeking asylum without taking them into the care of the local authority and affording them a service as 'looked after' children. This issue was mainly, but not exclusively, confined to children who arrived in the United Kingdom to seek asylum after they turned 16 years of age.

A report produced by the Audit Commission in 2000 first drew attention to this issue and noted that:

> In many cases, they do not receive the same standard of care routinely afforded to indigenous children in need, even though their legal rights are identical. Many authorities, for example, do not offer 16 and 17 year-old unaccompanied children a full needs assessment, and the commission's survey found that only one-third had individual care plans in place for those in their care. (Audit Commission, 2000: 66)

In the same year, research by Barnardo's, which explored the nature of social work services to these children and young people, found that 'Local Authorities mainly provide services under Section 17 of the Children Act 1989, which is designed to offer support to families where there are children in need' (Stone, 2000: 4).

This was still the case in 2002; a monitoring project conducted by The Children's Society, Save the Children and the Refugee Council identified widespread use of section 17 to support unaccompanied children seeking asylum, in some cases without the needs of individual children being assessed in line with government policy. The study also looked at problems with social work support as reported by children and young people. It found that 'Those young people reporting that they "only see a social worker to collect money/vouchers" or "have no allocated social worker" were more likely to be supported under section 17' (Dennis, 2002: 11).

This reveals something of the nature of support given to many unaccompanied children at the time, as well as the legal framework under which it was provided. More recently, the true complexity of the range of quality in social work was highlighted (Wade et al., 2005). However, this study also drew attention to this same issue; the research cited the following explanation from a social worker: 'The provision of services under section 17 of the Children Act 1989 was "standard practice; it was actually part of the assessment form"' (Wade et al., 2005: 53). It appeared that policy was being developed from social work managers rather than from national guidance. In 2001, Save the Children (Stanley, 2001) found that, in almost all of the social work teams included within its study, 16- and 17-year olds would be taken into the looked after system only in exceptional circumstances. In effect, this amounted to a policy, whether written or not, which dictated that services be provided based on age rather than assessed needs (Stanley, 2001: 37).

Two developments in 2002 and 2003 were influential in changing this approach. The first was an amendment to the 1989 Act made through section 116 of the Adoption and Children Act 2002. It was introduced as a response to court cases unrelated to unaccompanied children seeking asylum, and had the ironic effect of introducing legislative change that most social work practitioners had understood to be already enshrined in law. The amendment allowed local authorities to provide accommodation under section 17 of the 1989 Act, without automatically making a child looked after. Prior to this amendment, regardless of the intentions of a local authority, if accommodation had been provided as part of a social work response this would have resulted in those children legally being seen as looked after.

This issue was clarified in 'R (on the application of Berhe and others) v Hillingdon London Borough Council'. This judgement, commonly referred to as the Hillingdon judgement, confirmed that the applicants, by virtue of being provided with accommodation as part of the social work service, were 'looked after' and any attempt by the local authority to distinguish between sections 17 and 20 was 'mere sophistry'. This was an important test case that established the legislative context for those children supported by social services prior to introduction of the Adoption and Children Act on 7 November 2002. After this date local authority social services departments could legally provide services including accommodation to unaccompanied children under section 17 of the 1989 Act.

However, in June 2003, guidance issued by the Department of Health gave an important steer to social workers assessing the needs of unaccompanied children seeking asylum and making decisions about the level of care and support that these children and young people should be afforded. A local authority circular (Department of Health, 2003: 13) explained the legal situation following the amendment to section 17, and offered the following guidance:

> where a child has no parent or guardian in this country, perhaps because he has arrived alone seeking asylum, the presumption should be that he would fall within the scope of section 20 and become looked after, unless the needs assessment reveals particular factors which would suggest that an alternative response would be more appropriate.

Subsequent briefings and studies have sought to explain this situation to social work practitioners (Refugee Council, 2003) and comment on how widely the policy is being implemented (Dennis, 2005; Free, 2005).

The scope of the 1989 Act's remit towards unaccompanied children seeking asylum remains the cause of much comment. The reasons for this may be complex and include political and/or resource concerns, as well as misunderstanding of the legislation and policy context. Social workers themselves have expressed concern:

> There has always been a policy vacuum around whether they are to be treated as children and the Children Act be paramount, or are they to be treated as migrants and the Immigration Act be paramount. That's the big one, that's the one that needs to be answered. (Free, 2005: 35)

If the 1989 Act itself makes no reference to excluding unaccompanied children from its remit and guidance specifically includes them, how has this perceived 'conflict' arisen? Many commentators cite the limited commitment made by the UK government to the United Nations Convention on the Rights of the Child. Ayotte and Williamson (2001) list it as one of the 'obstacles to ... realising the rights of separated children' (69).

The impact of the reservation on the UN Convention on the Rights of the Child

The UK government entered the following reservation when it ratified the Convention on the Rights of the Child (CRC) in December 1991:

> The United Kingdom reserves the right to apply such legislation, in so far as it relates to the entry into, stay in and departure from the United Kingdom of those who do not have the right under the law of the United Kingdom to enter and remain in the United Kingdom, and to the acquisition and possession of citizenship, as it may deem necessary from time to time.

The Committee on the Rights of the Child has declared this reservation incompatible with the object and purposes of the CRC. It has received widespread criticism by children's rights organisations. In 2001, Save the Children (Blake and Drew, 2001) obtained a legal opinion on this incompatibility; which also explored the extent to which the reservation improperly restricts application of the CRC in the United Kingdom and concluded that 'In its present form the Reservation lends itself to a broad meaning and has been so applied by domestic courts' (2). And, furthermore that 'The maintenance of the Reservation to the CRC gives rise to the wrong implication that the "best interests" principle may be excluded wholesale from areas of executive discretion concerned with immigration, asylum and nationality' (2). It appears, therefore, that there is general consensus that the reservation on the CRC should have no impact on social work services for unaccompanied children seeking asylum. However, it is also widely believed that in practice, its impact is far reaching: 'It should not limit the application of other rights set out in the CRC but it is frequently misinterpreted to limit the application of the provisions of the CRC to other aspects of a child's life if he or she is subject to immigration control' (Crawley, 2004: 31). This is still refuted by government. In a parliamentary debate in 2005, the spokesperson for the government, Baroness Andrew, responded to criticism from parliamentary colleagues:

> First of all, let us be clear about the reservation. I am sorry but, as the noble Lord anticipated, I cannot give a commitment to lift the reservation. It is for the wider policy in relation to immigration. But we adhere to the spirit of the convention in the formulation of policy and procedure in relation to refugee and asylum-seeking children. We always seek to improve on what we do. I take the criticisms that have been made, but we take our responsibilities towards that group of vulnerable and traumatised children very seriously. (Hansard, 23 March 2005: Vol. 671, pt. 58, col. GC165)

This may seem to be borne-out in more recently published guidance whilst not specified in the legislation itself.

Guidance to the Children (Leaving Care) Act 2000 contains a short section on the remit of the 1989 Act towards unaccompanied children. It includes a useful summary of the government's position:

> Unaccompanied asylum-seeking children (UASC) are covered by the Children Act 1989 and the new provisions introduced by the Children (Leaving Care) Act in exactly the same way as other children in this country. However, they will also have an immigration status – applying for asylum, acceptance as a refugee, granted exceptional leave to remain or refused leave to remain – which will need to be taken into account by councils providing services to them. (Department of Health, 2001: 13)

This statement appears to contain within it the very incompatibility that social work practitioners have been struggling with. On the one hand, the children and young people are to be assessed and given a social work service under the same law and policy as children and young people who are UK citizens, but social work practitioners must take account of the immigration status of every child and provide a service relevant to that status. What does this mean? It may refer to the nature of the service provided. Indeed, as discussed above, guidance that has been written with these children in mind has always referred to their particular vulnerability or additional needs. The government, however, appear to be saying more than this – the above statement talks specifically about 'immigration status', not their background and needs.

Further evidence that this may be the case may be found in the Green Paper *Care Matters: Transforming the Lives of Children and Young People in Care* (DfES, 2006). The first specific mention of unaccompanied children seeking asylum is in the first chapter: 'This group of children often have different needs to other children in care, which will be looked at in more detail in a forthcoming consultation to be published by the Home Office.' In response to the Children's Commissioner for England who had asked for clarification, the Secretary of State for Education stated that

> I am happy to assure you that [UASC] will benefit from the Green Paper as a whole, not only from the proposals targeted specifically at them. As you know, there are some particular issues for this group, the majority of whom return home to their country of origin at some point. They and their carers often need help and support in understanding the asylum process, in order to prepare for a positive return home where appropriate. Beyond these particular needs though, this is a group of children like any other, and should receive the same excellent support from the Local Authority (LA) as corporate parents that we would expect for any child in care.

How far then, does the asylum legal and policy framework affect social work services to unaccompanied children seeking asylum?

Guiding principles of immigration and asylum policy

The principles currently guiding government policy on asylum can be found in the five-year strategy for asylum and immigration published in February 2005. The strategy's title *Controlling our borders; making migration work for Britain* may reveal something of its guiding principles but they are spelt out within the document itself:

> This five-year plan for our immigration and asylum system ... shows how we are going to enforce strict controls to root out abuse. It will ensure Britain continues to benefit from people from abroad who work hard and add to our prosperity. And, importantly, it puts forward solutions to a difficult issue, which are clear, workable and in the best interests of this country. (5)

Whilst the strategy document relates to immigration and asylum, this chapter is only concerned with the principles and policies relating to asylum. In the foreword to the document, which is provided by the Prime Minister, Tony Blair, the word 'abuse' appears several times relating to the asylum system. Both this section and the foreword by the Secretary of State use the term 'genuine refugees'. This underlines the principles stated at the beginning of the document; immigration control is about strengthening borders and the role of the Immigration and Nationality Directorate is to sift out those who try to abuse the asylum system and ensure they do not stay in the United Kingdom, whilst at the same time welcoming those who need to be here because they are fleeing persecution and need a 'safe haven'.

Recent legislative changes are compatible with this approach. Whilst legislative and policy change as far back as 1996 could be cited as relevant to the picture that we have today, for the purposes of this chapter I will look at those elements of policy development that have had the biggest direct impact on social services for unaccompanied children. This discussion will focus on three policy areas arising out of asylum law and policy and explore the implications for social work with unaccompanied children seeking asylum.

Temporary leave

The government is able to use its discretion to allow people to remain in the country outside the immigration rules. This may be necessary when the government deems it either unsafe or inappropriate to expect applicants to return to their country of origin, even when it is deemed that they do not meet the criteria for refugee status as defined in article 1 (A) of the 1951 United Nations Convention Relating to the Status of Refugees. Few unaccompanied children in the United Kingdom are recognised as refugees and many are granted leave outside of the rules. Prior to 2003 this leave was called 'exceptional leave to remain'. In March 2003 the term 'discretionary leave' was introduced to describe leave given outside of the immigration rules.

In 2001, the government introduced a new policy, which afforded limited protection to asylum applicants who are unaccompanied children and whose claim for asylum has been refused. It stated those children aged between 14 and 17 for whom reception arrangements cannot be made in their homeland would only be granted exceptional leave to remain until their eighteenth birthday. This was a significant policy shift and underlined the government's view that protection would only be afforded to children for as long as they are children. As soon as they reach 18 they will be immediately treated as adults and therefore only given protection in line with policies for adults.

In 2004, another policy further limited the length of time that some children were to be granted leave outside of the immigration rules, the status by this time called discretionary leave. It was to apply to unaccompanied children whose country of origin was on a list that had been introduced into legislation through section 94 of the Nationality, Immigration and Asylum Act 2002. Unaccompanied children seeking asylum from one of these designated countries, if refused, were to be granted discretionary leave of 12 months, or until their eighteenth birthday, whichever is the shorter. At the time of announcement there were nine countries on this list, but it is subject to change. The announcement of this policy gave advanced notice of a related policy that was to be announced in the five-year strategy *Controlling our borders; making migration work for Britain*.

Returns of unaccompanied children

The five-year strategy brought official notification of an intention to develop an enforced-removal programme for unaccompanied children whose asylum applications have been refused:

> We will address the difficult issue of returning **unaccompanied asylum seeking children**. The key is to trace their families in their countries of origin or to create other acceptable reception arrangements. We are beginning a project in Albania. We do not believe that it is in a child's best interests to remain in the UK separated from their parents or communities. (Home Office, 2005: 31)

There is little detail here and no new policy or process documents have been made public, although some relevant stakeholders have been in regular contact with the Immigration and Nationality Directorate regarding progress on its plans. These stakeholders have included representatives from local authority social services departments, although many social work practitioners remain confused about the programme and their role within it.

Transition at 18

This policy, also related to those already mentioned as turning 18 years of age, has become a bigger issue since the introduction of a policy granting leave up until an unaccompanied child's eighteenth birthday. Prior to that, it mainly affected young people whose asylum claim had received no initial decision and had not been looked after by a local authority, as they were transferred into the adult support system on their eighteenth birthday. At the time this policy was introduced in 2000, this resulted in young people being moved from a placement provided by social services to a system of voucher support and accommodation in a dispersal area. It was a source of considerable distress for young people:

> There is considerable confusion, anxiety and a lack of information about what happens to a young person when they reach 18 years. A number of professionals pointed

to the potentially disastrous effects of the transition to adult systems at 18, especially dispersal, which entails the loss of friends, support and even homelessness. (Stanley, 2001: 68)

This highlights the complex relationship between the issue highlighted earlier of support under section 17 being commonplace at this time and the separate system of support offered to asylum seekers over the age of 18. Social work practitioners who had made the decision to provide a minimal level of support to an unaccompanied child under section 17 of the Children Act 1989 found themselves advocating for those same young people not to be dispersed under the adult support system when they turned 18.

More recently the issue has changed. Whilst not all, many more young people are now eligible for continued social work provision beyond their eighteenth birthday, as care leavers. Dennis (2005: 7) noted that

it is clear that many changes have been made. Senior managers and, in some cases, legal departments and directors of social services have been involved in decisions aimed at improving the service to children and young people. This indicates that some notice has been taken of the guidance issued in LAC (2003) 13 as well as the Hillingdon judgement.

However, changes to legislation made in the Nationality, Immigration and Asylum Act 2002 have limited the support that local authorities may provide to certain classes of people, including those who came to the United Kingdom to seek asylum. Recent developments have indicated its possible impact upon leaving care services to former unaccompanied children who claimed asylum before they were 18.

Section 54 and Schedule 3 of the Nationality, Immigration and Asylum Act 2002 came into force in January 2003. This Act has the effect of preventing local authorities from providing support to certain classes of people, including European Economic Area (EEA) nationals (other than the United Kingdom) and persons with refugee status in another EEA state. The two classes of person defined in Schedule 3 that are relevant to those who sought asylum as unaccompanied children are

- persons unlawfully present in the United Kingdom who are not asylum seekers
- failed asylum seekers who refuse to co-operate with removal directions.

Guidance issued by the Home Office to local authorities and housing authorities immediately prior to implementation (December 2002) included a paragraph on 'Former Unaccompanied Asylum Seeking Children'. It states that

Unaccompanied Asylum Seeker Children are normally granted exceptional leave until the age of 18. If, upon reaching 18 the individual applies for asylum, NASS will normally provide support (depending on the date the person applied for asylum). If such an individual becomes a failed asylum seeker then they should be treated in the same way as any other asylum seeker as regards asylum support (ie., support will be withdrawn). In addition if they become a failed asylum seeker and fail to comply with removal directions then any assistance being provided by a local authority under the provisions of the Children Act 1989 must be withdrawn. Such individuals can leave the UK either through removal by the Immigration Service or through a voluntary departure with VARP [the Voluntary Assisted Returns Programme]. (Home Office, undated: para 26)

Practice developed in accordance with this guidance, which was interpreted by practitioners to mean that young people who are care leavers and who applied for asylum as unaccompanied children may be provided with support under the 1989 Act until they fail to comply with removal directions issued to them.

In November 2004, direct communication to various stakeholders, including the Association of Directors of Social Services, indicated that the Home Office were at this point interpreting Schedule 3 differently. The letter advises that 'in respect of former unaccompanied asylum-seeking children, consideration needs to be given to paragraph 7 of Schedule 3 – "person unlawfully in United Kingdom" – the fourth class of ineligible person.'

It goes on to outline various different scenarios that may apply to such young people. For those who had been granted a period of leave that expired on their eighteenth birthday and who had been refused any further leave and associated appeals, it is asserted that 'he will be in the UK unlawfully within the paragraph of Schedule 3'. It then advises that support may only be provided under sections 23C, 24A or 24B of the Children Act 1989, unless it is necessary to provide support for the purpose of avoiding a breach of a person's rights under the European Convention on Human Rights (ECHR).

The Home Office subsequently informed stakeholders that they intended to issue new guidance accordingly, and in 2005 established a working party to consider options for support for care leavers affected by this interpretation of Schedule 3.

The implications of asylum law and policy on social work with unaccompanied children seeking asylum

The impact of guiding principles is hard to measure yet it may be asserted that it is here that the greatest effect is made. It is, as has already been outlined, fundamental to the Children Act 1989 and policies that follow, that children's views must be heard and considered. In 1999, Amnesty International reported on the treatment of unaccompanied children seeking asylum and concluded that children do not fully participate in decisions made by the Immigration and Nationality Directorate that affect them. In terms of impact on social work services, it may be useful to distinguish between those provided with services as looked after children and care leavers over the age of 18.

Looked after children

As outlined already, children are often given a period of temporary leave to remain in the United Kingdom. This can be as little as a few weeks, and is frequently less than three years. The effects of this on permanency planning are obvious, as outlined by BAAF. 'The complex circumstances of unaccompanied children especially those connected to their asylum application and their family circumstances make establishing permanent placements particularly challenging. ... instability and uncertainty and possibility of a "failed" asylum claim are never far away' (BAAF, 2006: 3).

Care planning should not be dependent on certainty, as plans should be flexible and allow for a range of options for the future. In theory, a social work practitioner can make a 'dual' plan, one route if the child is allowed to stay and an alternative should they be required to return to their country of origin. In practice, however, there are many possible options, including prolonged periods of uncertainty, particularly with regard to timing of events that fall within the remit of a separate executive.

Even whilst the child is in the care of social services, the influence of the Immigration and Nationality Directorate is great. This chapter has looked at the use of sections 17 and 20 to support unaccompanied children seeking asylum and the extent to which unwritten policies have influenced differences in services based on age. This is influenced by the levels of funding provided to local authorities by the Immigration and Nationality Directorate, which are differential according to the age of the young person. It is impossible to make general statements about the actual impact on services but social work practitioners and managers report this differential, and the unrealistically low amounts provided, as significant. As Free (2005) reports, whilst the Home Office states that the grant is designed to contribute towards the costs, the reality for most social workers is that they have to provide an entire social work service within the grant allowance. One interviewee states that 'it goes against everything you know about good practice' (Free, 2005: 32).

The impact at a strategic level may therefore be considerable. There is a lack of knowledge about what the future holds – which is related to the numbers of new arrivals, possible changes to policies relating to funding, as well as cases such as the Hillingdon judgement that may influence a service as a result of clarification of social work duties under the 1989 Act and Children (Leaving Care) Act 2000. This does of course affect personal social work with individual children and young people. Funding restraints will influence the choice of placements and the numbers of children and young people on a social work practitioner's caseload, which will have an impact on their capacity to meet the number and variety of needs presented. Wade et al. (2005: 220) spoke to social work practitioners who reported such an effect: 'I just don't think we the social workers have the time, given the caseloads we have, to do what we would like to do with these children.'

However, as has been noted by many commentators, the response to unaccompanied children by social work practitioners can vary within teams and cannot be entirely explained by external factors (Wade et al., 2005; Kohli, 2006).

Free (2005) provides a useful summary of the barriers identified by social work practitioners and managers to providing the quality of looked after service that is deemed necessary. Some barriers are related to funding, others relate to staff attitudes and capabilities or the support of senior managers. But, it is also important to see social work with these children and young people within the context of all social work, where some of the same difficulties are encountered. A helpful summary of recent difficulties may be seen in reports of the Commission for Social Care Inspection, including *Making Every Child Matter* (CSCI, 2005). These difficulties include a shortage of social workers, limited placement choice and a lack of consistency in responses to referrals.

It may be argued, then, that a looked after service to unaccompanied children seeking asylum will have certain constraints placed upon it, which may affect the quality of social work service a practitioner is able to provide. However, these external factors combine with other issues, including the different ways individual practitioners respond to need and how committed they are to providing a supportive environment for the children and young people for whom they are responsible. As Kohli (2000: 7) explains

> Good social work practice means finding ... a balance between the universal and specific needs of their charges. It means not splitting unaccompanied children into deserving and undeserving, good or bad. It means taking a sensitively forensic approach to their burdens, neither rushing for information, nor denying its importance in terms of planning. It also means providing connections at a level that is tolerable and meaningful for each child.

Care leavers over the age of 18

For those children whose care experience results in them becoming former relevant children under the Children (Leaving Care) Act 2000, the duties towards them by local authorities are outlined in the said Act and its guidance. As already stated, this guidance was clear about its remit towards unaccompanied children at the time of publication. However, as outlined above, Schedule 3 of the Nationality, Immigration and Asylum Act 2002 limits the provision of social work service to those young people who, as a result of the decision to refuse to grant further discretionary leave after their leave upto age18 has expired, are referred to as persons unlawfully present in the United Kingdom. The test of what support may be given under Schedule 3, in order to avoid a breach of a young person's rights under the European Convention on Human

Rights (ECHR) has not yet been tried by the judiciary, although a related case indicates that a service may only be provided to the extent to which a breach of those rights may be avoided. In the case of AW v London Borough of Croydon (2005) EWHC 2950, the judge ruled that

> the effect of paragraph 3 of Schedule 3 is that if a breach of human rights would otherwise result, a public body with power to act must exercise that power in order to avoid such a breach. However, the duty that arises can be no more than a duty to exercise a power in accordance with its terms. (para 50)

This case was not addressing the duties of a local authority under the Children Act 1989, so it is important that we do not make assumptions about its applicability to former unaccompanied children. For these young people the impact of immigration legislation and policy is potentially of great significance. Broadly speaking, a young person's immigration status at age 18 will determine the likely impact of Schedule 3, although the detail of this impact will depend upon the outcome of future policy decisions and associated guidance to local authorities.

In general, the major factor influencing social work with former relevant children and young people who were unaccompanied children seeking asylum is the perspective from the Home Office that once 18, such individuals can be treated as adults. This means therefore, that they are subject to policies that as children they were excluded or protected from. Schedule 3 is one such policy – social work provision under section 20 of the Children Act 1989 is excluded from its remit. In a similar way, just as the Home Office exempts unaccompanied children from detention, or requires that enforced removal may only take place once safe reception and care arrangements have been made, these policies end on the young person's eighteenth birthday. This has a huge impact on the young person, as has been documented in Stanley (2001) and Dennis (2002) amongst others.

Recommendations for practice in this area have emerged more recently in Free (2006) and Wade et al. (2005), as well as in the guide to transitions written by the Association of Directors of Social Services (ADSS, 2005) together with a multi-agency advisory group. These documents largely concentrate on forward planning, keeping the young person informed at all stages and communicating with other relevant professionals and agencies. Another aspect of the work that is seen to be helpful is the practical support that social work practitioners can offer, when a young person is facing detention and/or enforced removal. The advice given by Free (2006: 12–16) and the ADSS guide both include practical steps that can be taken with a view to both exploring all the possible outcomes at a time of crisis in the young person's journey. This action may consist of two distinct stages. First, the social work practitioner can be the 'key' contact for all agencies that may need to be contacted to ensure that the proposed action is lawful and cannot be challenged. Second, once it is established that the young person will be detained or removed, the social work practitioner can be the main source of emotional and practical support. This may include visiting the young person, arranging for his/her belongings to be collected and taken to the person, and listening to his/her thoughts and fears.

Through this practice, for example, social work practitioners may be returning to the role defined at the beginning of this chapter. At a Refugee Council conference workshop in 2005 practitioners reported feelings of anger and powerlessness that were felt to reflect the response of many of the young people in this situation. However, it can be argued that such practitioners are providing an invaluable resource to the young person and, at a time of crisis, using their skills as problem solvers and intervention in order to effect change as embodied in the definitions of social work cited above.

References

ADSS. (2005). *Key transitions for unaccompanied asylum seeking children. Guidance for social workers, personal advisers and their managers working with unaccompanied asylum seeking children.* (Available online: http://www.adss.org.uk/publications/guidance/transitions.pdf).

Audit Commission. (2000). *Another Country: Implementing Dispersal under the Immigration and Asylum Act 1999.* London: Audit Commission for Local Authorities and the National Health Service in England and Wales.

Ayotte, W. and Williamson, L. (2001). *Separated Children in the UK: An overview of the Current Situation.* London: Refugee Council and Save the Children.

BAAF. (2006). *Permanency Planning for Unaccompanied Asylum Seeking Children in England and Wales.* London: BAAF.

BASW. (2002). *Code of Ethics for Social Work.* Birmingham: British Association of Social Workers.

Blake, N. and Drew, S. (2001). *In the Matter of the United Kingdom Reservation to the UN Convention on the Rights of the Child.* London: Save the Children.

The Children's Legal Centre. (2003). *Mapping the Provision of Education and Social Services For Refugee and Asylum Seeker Children: Lessons from the Eastern Region.* Cambridge: The Children's Legal Centre, The University of Essex.

Commission for Social Care Inspection. (2005). *Making Every Child Matter: Messages from Inspections of Children's Social Services.* London: The Stationery Office.

Crawley, H. (2004). *Working with Children and Young People Subject to Immigration Control: Guidelines for Best Practice.* London: Immigration Law Practitioners Association.

Dennis, J. (2002). *A Case for Change: How Refugee Children in England Are Missing Out.* London: Save the Children, Refugee Council and The Children's Society.

——. (2005). *Ringing the Changes: The Impact of Guidance on the Use of Sections 17 and 20 of the Children Act 1989 to Support Unaccompanied Asylum-Seeking Children.* London: Refugee Council.

Department for Education and Skills. (2003). *Every Child Matters.* (Available online: http://www.everychildmatters.gov.uk/).

——. (2006). *Care matters: Transforming the lives of children and young people in care,* Cm 6932, 2006) (Available online: http://www.dfes.gov.uk/consultations/conResults.cfm?consultationId=1406).

Department of Health. (1995). *Unaccompanied Asylum Seeking Children: A Practice Guide*. London: Department of Health.

——. (2001). *Children (Leaving Care) Act 2000: Regulations and Guidance*. London: Department of Health.

——. (2003). Guidance on accommodating children in need and their families. Local Authority Circular, 2 June 2003, *LAC*, (2003)13. (Available online: http://www.dh. gov.uk/assetRoot/04/01/27/56/04012756.pdf).

Department of Health, Department for Education and Employment, Home Office. (2000). *Framework for the Assessment of Children in Need and Their Families*. London: The Stationery Office.

Free, E. (2005). *Local Authority Support to Unaccompanied Asylum Seeking Young People: Changes since the Hillingdon Judgement*. London: Save the Children.

——. (2006). *Unaccompanied Refugees and Asylum Seekers Turning 18: A Guide for Social Workers and Other Professionals*. London: Save the Children.

Home Office. (2005). *Controlling Our Borders: Making Migration Work for Britain*. London: The Stationery Office.

Home Office Immigration and Nationality Directorate. (Undated). *Nationality, Immigration and Asylum Act 2002 Section 54 and Schedule 3 and the Withholding and Withdrawal of Support (Travel Assistance and Temporary Accommodation) Regulations 2002: Guidance to Local Authorities and Housing Authorities*. (Available online: http://www.asylumsupport.info/guidance.pdf).

——. (2004). *APU notice 5/2004 Application of Non Suspensive Appeal (NSA) Process to Asylum Seeking Children*. (Available online: www.ind.homeoffice.gov.uk).

Kidane, S. (2001). *Food, Shelter and Half a Chance: Assessing the Needs of Unaccompanied Asylum Seeking and Refugee Children*. London: BAAF.

Kohli, R. K. S. (2000). Issues for social work with unaccompanied asylum seeking children, *Professional Social Work: The Magazine of the British Association of Social Workers*, June 2002: 6–9.

——. (2006). The sound of silence: listening to what unaccompanied asylum seeking children say and do not say, *British Journal of Social Work*, 36: 707–721.

R. (AW and others) v London Borough of Croydon and others (QBD) [2005] EWHC 2950 (QB).

——. (Helen Berhe, Yorsmame Kidane, Wahdat Munir, Albertina Ncube) v Hillingdon London Borough Council [2003] EWHC 2075 (Admin).

Refugee Council. (2003). *Support Arrangements for 16 to 17 Year Old Unaccompanied Asylum Seeking Children*. London: Refugee Council.

Stanley, K. (2001). *Cold Comfort: Young Separated Refugees in England*. London: Save the Children.

Stone, R. (2000). *Children First and Foremost: Meeting The Needs of Unaccompanied Asylum Seeking Children*. Barkingside: Barnardos.

Wade, J., Mitchell, F. and Baylis, G. (2005). *Unaccompanied Asylum Seeking Children: The Response of Social Work Services*. London: BAAF.

CHAPTER 3

Practitioner Stories

Ravi K. S. Kohli

Introduction

Social Workers, like asylum seekers, sometimes appear to stand in public esteem on the margins of respectability. In a territory that is ambivalent or one in which commentators are poorly informed about the demands of day-to-day practice, there is a tendency to shunt images of social workers into easy and negative compartments – incompetent, bureaucratic, controlling, permissive, abusive, 'politically correct', unskilled and lacking common sense, and so on (Ferguson, 2003). Within these labels, stories told about social work practice with unaccompanied minors are generally rather bleak (Stanley, 2001; Humphries, 2004). The formula used by some commentators is simple. They begin with an image of unaccompanied minors as vulnerable and needy. They argue for better resources and practices to alleviate need. They find that social services are poor, disorganised or defensive. They make recommendations for change. There is a confirmation of deficit and it is perhaps unsurprising that when looking for problems, problems are found and manipulated into shapes that give simple messages of need and blame that can rub out the complex lived realities that are part of everyday practice. Social workers are said to fail these children at a number of levels, both organisationally and in direct practice. For example, assessments of their needs are described as rather rudimentary, and the provision of care as a lottery, with a few winners amongst many losers (Kohli, 2007).

This chapter provides a contrast to this view based on a study that examined and attempted to develop a detailed understanding of what social workers do in practice with unaccompanied minors and why they do what they do. These lesser known aspects of contemporary social work are illustrated using some reflective accounts by practitioners. These stories both confirm the difficulties and dilemmas that social workers face in working with unaccompanied minors, as well as establish the ways in which good practice is delivered, often in turbulent circumstances. In all, 35 social workers were interviewed in four local authority Social Services Departments in England. Each of the workers was asked to tell the story of their work with one unaccompanied minor, and to think openly about the ways in which their work had shaped the process of resettlement for that minor.

Gathering stories of practice with unaccompanied minors

LeCroy (2002: 6) observes in his detailed study of why people become social workers and the sense they make of their own practice that one of the main points of such research is 'to enter and understand the everyday lived world of the social worker and his or her relation to it'. In doing so, I wanted to try and understand the possibilities, constraints, dilemmas and hopes the social workers experienced as part of their day-to-day practice. I also wanted to avoid 'advocacy research'. Jacobson and Landau (2003: 2), in a paper discussing research into refugee lives, are sharply critical of a researcher who

> already knows what s/he wants to see and say, and comes away from the research having 'proved' it. Although those falling into this trap are often well meaning, this kind of research risks doing refugees a disservice [and] encourages widespread acceptance of unsubstantiated facts that bolster a sense of permanent crisis and disaster.

Particularly in reference to social work, replication of an advocacy perspective built into the structure and process of the research could have risked another voice discussing how poor practice was leading to poor outcomes for the young people, or indeed how maligned practitioners were as they struggled to do their jobs. I did not consider it necessary to 'highlight new and different ways refugees have become victims' (Jacobson and Landau, 2003: 19) or indeed how practitioners were being victimised themselves or acting in oppressive ways. Rather, I wanted to minimise bias while recognising that neutrality in any absolute sense is not possible to claim within a naturalistic enquiry. Similarly, while I was conscious that social work practice was in some way reported in a shallow manner, neither did I want to champion the cause of social work. In applying Dingwall's (1980) advice for ethnographers, it was clear that 'The desire to champion the underdog is inimical to [an enquiry] whose claims to be distinguishable from polemic or investigative journalism must rely on an ability to comprehend the perspectives of top dogs, bottom dogs, and indeed lap dogs' (quoted in Spencer et al., 2003: 66).

This notion of comprehending a variety of perspectives would not have been possible from an advocacy point of view. Rather, I wanted to ensure that there was depth and breadth to the perspectives that were seen and that these dimensions could be viewed from as neutral a position as possible rather than arranged hierarchically by counter-pointing my 'good' position in relation to others' 'bad' positions. I also wanted to take account, as a researcher, of issues related to trust and mistrust in research related to refugees and their helpers (Hynes, 2003). Daniel and Knudson (1995: 1) assert that 'from its inception the experience of a refugee puts trust on trial. The refugee mistrusts and is mistrusted.' A number of researchers comment on this phenomenon, and how difficult it is on this basis to engage with refugees particularly when distrust is, for them, a functional aspect of existence (Robinson and Segrott, 2002). Similarly, for practitioners struggling with how to establish trust with an unaccompanied minor, where open, 'truthful' dialogue was less likely to exist than a cautious rehearsed story, I was aware that the ripples of distrust could move in all directions, leading to practitioners themselves feeling protective of their own stories when faced with a researcher. In these instances, where the lack of trust serves a purpose within the system that a researcher enters, Lee (1993: 208) notes that the establishment of trust in any sensitive area of research enquiry 'depends on the quality of the interpersonal engagement between the researcher and the researched and the building over the course of the research relationship of increasing levels of fellowship, mutual self-disclosure and reciprocity'. While I would caution against assuming a simple meaning for terms such as 'self-disclosure' 'reciprocity' and 'fellowship' within a research relationship, at times during the interviews with the social workers I recognised some of the dilemmas that practitioners faced as they described the raw nature of some of their work, and felt sad at some stories and uplifted by others. Part of the process of undertaking the research interviews was about listening in a heartfelt manner to the respondents, but remaining neutral, very much like a therapeutic engagement. I never talked about myself, or allowed their story to be displaced by mine, but fellowship in the sense of joining around an issue of common interest was part of the process. It was also very helpful that I had myself been a local authority social worker for a number of years, and being able to 'belong' to a community of workers in this way, speaking the language they spoke, and understanding their responsibilities within the local authority context helped to settle some of the sensitivities. Following on from the issue of trust and distrust, I also wanted to understand the stories that were told *to* the social workers by the young people and the types of stories they then told about their own practice, from as many perspectives as possible. As I have described elsewhere (Kohli, 2007), telling 'thin' stories – that is, stories that maximise their chance for status and are designed to fit into the narrow legal criteria by which status is defined in the country of application – has a *purpose* for refugees, in the same way that the maintenance of distrust can be functional, but the consequence of doing so is to hide individual 'thicker stories' that tell of life 'in the round'. This phenomenon, from a research methodology perspective, is dwelt on by Bertrand (2000), in what he terms 'the autobiographical method of investigating the psychosocial wellness of refugees'. When gathering refugee stories, he suggests that the researcher is empathic and non-directive, even if the contrived story that the refugee tells is a mask that is presented to the researcher in the same way that it is 'to any figure perceived to be in authority'. He notes (Bertrand, 2000: 96) that

> Throughout their lives, refugees have hidden a certain part of their story, or highlighted their professional experiences (in order to be selected) or persecutions (in

order to get refugee status), **in an imaginary and creative way** [emphasis added] and even ... social workers find it difficult to get a story that remains the same (names, relatives, events might change over time).

This description of why stories are told in the ways that they are links well in methodological terms with the notion of getting to 'thick description' via a naturalistic study as developed within ethnography by Geertz (1973). Seale (1999: 94) gives a succinct account of this approach as 'Revealing and build-ing on many-layered interpretations of social life, so that a rich and detailed understanding of the **several meanings available for particular events** is pos-sible. Thin description, on the other hand, fails to engage with cultural mean-ings, and is both uninspired and uninspiring [emphasis added].'

It follows that thick and thin stories can have thick or thin descriptions, and that the measure of a good naturalistic enquiry is to see how, for example, thick descriptions are given of 'thin' phenomena. In terms of this enquiry, hav-ing a chance to first of all record the layers of stories known to social workers created the possibility of seeing whether I could come up with thick descrip-tions of the different stories that the young people were telling their workers. The design of this study also created the possibility of asking social workers how they came to know and believe in the stories that the young people told them, and whether they themselves appraised these stories in creative and opti-mistic ways. Here, the idea was to see whether the practitioners had multiple interpretations of the stories they were told. The stories were gathered using an extensive interview schedule that contained three main research questions regarding social work practice:

- What social workers knew about the young people's lives, particularly in context of silence, secrets and mistrust being prevalent?
- How social workers understood the notion of resettlement and described the ways they helped unaccompanied minors to resettle?
- Overall, how they experienced the young people and what sense they made of their own relationships with them?

As the interviews progressed, it became clear that the stories that the respondents told were a patchwork of facts, gaps and suppositions, and that these elements could be thought about purposefully – that is to say that what was known *and* not known were equally meaningful in terms of the whole emer-gent picture. Many of the respondents were surprised at how little they knew about the pre-departure 'ordinary' lives of the young people, as if the interview itself had given them a chance to take stock of this gap in understanding. As a small yet important example of this, when asked whether the young person had brought a memento of any sort from their earlier lives, the respondents were able to think about the meaning of the presence or absence of a memento, and what it might be like to have come away from family without, for example, a photograph or keepsake. Simultaneously, they were able to consider whether they had ever thought about asking the young person about this, or seen any item that was brought from home, and what their own asking or not asking indicated about their practice. Similarly, those who had spent much of their energy on focusing on the day-to-day 'real' demands from the young people, realised that 'forgetting' about key issues such as reunification or repatriation revealed not just the absence of planning in relation to key elements of the young person's future well-being, but also allowed them to reflect on why they might have forgotten, and how they would try to remember. A concrete result of such reflections was that in those instances where the social workers had no copy of the young person's asylum application to the Home Office, the respondents were able to plan how they would access a copy, with the young person's knowledge and consent. In exceptional cases, where there was a history of the young person having survived torture, stories were hard to tell, and drew on the respondents' capacities to put deep, complex and hard to manage feelings into words that attempted to preserve dignity, for themselves and the young person. These capacities reflected the broader attempt to turn experience into narrative, and bring order to what the respondents sometimes referred to as 'random acts of violence' that the young people had lived through.

Practitioner stories

The stories told by practitioners are organised here into three dimensions – told from the perspective of those workers who had a practical orientation to the work, those that worked with evocative feelings from the past and responded in an emotionally attuned way to the complex challenges faced by the minors, and those that had durable relationships with them, following them from uncertain beginnings in the United Kingdom to sustainable futures. Whichever of these dimensions the practitioners worked within, they did not find the work easy. In some respects they lived with doubt, ambiguity and fragmentation as did the minors themselves, and this uncertainty pitched them into using their wits and intelligence in ways that were attractive as well as exhausting, both intellectually and emotionally. Some of them stayed in the work because of these challenges. Others bordered on scepticism edged with a tired 'seen it all before' cynicism. Some found the children heart warming, and developed an affectionate relationship with them over time. Others did what was practically necessary in moving the case along towards resolution. Within these boundaries of proximity and distance, layered understandings and quick fixes, the social workers told their stories of practice and reflected on what they knew and did not know about the children and about themselves as practitioners.

Being trustworthy and reliable

SW: I think initially he felt quite worried about his [immigration] status and what we were going to do with the information that he would give us. I think it's only as he is seeing that in fact we will make plans for him to stay here that he's becoming a little bit more open about things. I think it's really about building up trust.

As noted above, when entering a territory where you are desperate to be accepted in relation to the claim that you make, who you trust and how much you trust them becomes a vivid feature of life for refugees, including refugee children.

The interviews with the social workers showed that they were attuned to the need to establish trust. For example, unaccompanied minors were perceived by them as crafting a story that allowed as easy an entry as possible into the United Kingdom. They said that stories were often told as a simple series of events, and that they had become used to hearing the same or similar stories form different children over time. The social workers' responses therefore contained two components – one was an attempt to make sense of the narratives of individual children from the child's point of view, and the other was to see how stories formed a pattern across children. This balancing of the singular with the general, incidents with patterns, became one way for some of the workers to remain both intrigued by and committed to the young person they were working with. There was some concern about 'crafty' stories – those that some practitioners felt were a confection of lies and half-truths – and in the main there was worry about how children holding synthetic stories could suffer by knowing something not to be true yet having to use it to forward their claims. They spoke of instances where, despite realising that lying, embellishment and half-truths served a purpose in preserving the hope of a successful asylum application, the children themselves became trapped in repetition, almost as if the more they told their made-up story and the more 'real' it became in their minds, the less they were able to recall the details of their ordinary lives before departure.

How could workers generate trust in these circumstances, where the children struggled with what to make visible, to whom, in what way, at what time? A minority of them remained distrusting themselves, reflecting the position of what Humphries (2004) has referred to as a preoccupation with acting as border guards to their own territories and resources. There was the ever present suspicion that the children were lying in order to get what they wanted, and that a bank of obfuscation had been created that could be hidden behind. The practitioners said that the cover often consisted of limited, reluctant or repetitive talk, of making phone calls to people not known to anyone in the formal network of care and protection, and of whispered, furtive attempts by older siblings to silence their younger brothers or sisters when facing questions about facts, places, names and dates of birth. In filling in the gaps in their knowledge about individual children, these social workers could make a grab for more general stereotypes, as in David's story below.

David's story of practical assistance

David had been qualified as a social worker for four years. He worked in a local authority Social Services Children and Families team in an inner city. He was the allocated worker for Leo, a 16-year old young man from an African country temporarily admitted to the United Kingdom while his asylum claim was considered. David said that the service he and others offered to unaccompanied minors was piecemeal, with little or no policy guidance or practical advice about best practice in relation to the needs of this group of children. He spoke of what he was 'required to do' in terms of linking to health and education resources, paying weekly allowances and finding suitable accommodation. He also felt 'completely ill-equipped' to work with asylum seekers, as he had received little training, and sensed that the rudimentary responses he made in the circumstances left Leo at a distance from him.

> I don't know how he fills his days. He doesn't have very much to say apart from asking for money. The problem with Leo is that like a lot of them, they [asylum seekers] sometimes come across as a bit aggressive, with a cold-blooded look and say 'I'm not leaving here until I get what I want' – it sounds very threatening and they can be very demanding.

David knew very little about Leo's family and his life before leaving his earlier home, or the events and circumstances that had led to his moving from the homeland. He noted that Leo had been consistently unwilling to give basic information about his family or his precise locality of origin. David did not know the parents' names, or any sense of favourite memories, events, or the things that Leo had experienced as sustaining in his childhood days. There was no record of Leo's educational or medical history, or religious affiliations. There was no account of trauma, or being witness to violence, and David had only the briefest, opaque understanding of the reasons for departure – whether family had been broken by successive waves of military assault through which Leo had become separated from his parents. David said that

> The soldiers from X took over or something and they [the family] had to go underground. It was political unrest and I think his family were in fear of their lives and his father could afford to get him out. It was a general thing about the soldiers bullying people from Leo's ethnic clan.

An older brother or cousin, David thought, had taken him to the country's border with enough money to buy a place in a lorry heading for Europe. The date of separation, and hence the length of time Leo had not seen his family, was unclear to David. As the interview progressed, David realised that fuzzy history was not something he would accept with indigenous children entering care, and that there was something about not knowing that perturbed him. He said

> I think you're asking me lots of searching questions and I think what is clear to me through this is that we've been very reactive to Leo's situation without being proactive about looking at history and what all that means and why he's here and what life was like. I feel we just go through this automatic 'Right, he's an asylum seeker,

let's accommodate him, give him a bit of money, do a medical screening, get him to school', and so on, and we rubber stamp him.

Here was an attempt by David to establish what he did not know and to make sense of not knowing. He realised he had created, with other colleagues, an internal border guard system for processing asylum seeking children, and that a bureaucratised approach to practice had led to a strained relationship with Leo. When asked to talk about how he himself experienced the relationship, David referred to it being

> Nothing very deep. Leo doesn't have very much to say other than ask for money. He just says he's alright, when I ask him how things are. I just see him when he comes in for his money. Probably the only thing he'd say about what I had done for him is that he's got somewhere to live and gets money each week.

As the interview progressed, I felt that there were many ways in which David appeared to underplay his importance to Leo. For example, David had made sure that Leo was cared for by someone who spoke his language of origin, who would keep up any cultural affiliations that Leo wanted to pursue. David knew that homeland food brought comfort to Leo and had made sure that a mini-fridge was brought to privately store ingredients that he could use to cook. Although Leo had expressed a wish not to join a mosque because he was worried about connecting with unsafe networks from the country of origin, David who had once unwittingly interrupted him at prayer, had brought him a prayer mat that could be used in his bedroom. David worried that Leo's will for an education was less powerful than his interest in earning money, and so had organised a small network of helpers – teaching assistants, teachers, other asylum seeking children in Leo's school – that had welcomed Leo into their territory, and helped him to learn English, to do his homework, and to keep up regular attendance at school. David knew that Leo liked predictability, so made sure the money supply remained uninterrupted and was regularly there each week on a Monday afternoon at 4 PM. Where possible, David said he ensured that Leo could have things to own. He knew that Leo had come with nothing but a small bag with a change of clothing – no mementos from home, or anything of enduring worth. So occasionally, David said he would present a case to his manager for extra money to buy a fleece, a cookbook, or more rarely a pair of trainers. He wanted Leo to be grateful for these efforts and resented what appeared to be a lack of grace by the young man, who could turn a wish into a demand, and a demand at times into a threat. Together, David and Leo maintained a distance, and from a distance focused on practicality.

Meera's story of the emotional content of the work

Meera's story, in comparison to David's, contained flecks of emotional colour from the start of the interview that grew bolder and deeper as the interview progressed. She chose to talk about her work with Lily, 17-years of age. Meera had been the allocated social worker for Lily for a year, and was the third social worker in the four years Lily had been in the care of Social Services. Meera knew details of Lily's life to a more precise degree than David had known about Leo. Lily, like Leo was from a country in Africa where war had obliterated civic life, and created many ghosts (Bracken and Petty, 1998). Lily had escaped with her adult half-sister to the United Kingdom. Meera knew that Lily's mother had died a few months after giving birth to her, so she had no conscious memory of being parented by her, depending instead on her sister's recollections. Meera described Lily as being very careful with showing her feelings, to a point where she felt Lily was nonchalant, hiding the impact of important experiences in ways that were functional and burdensome. Lily was seen by many people to be practical, tidy and careful.

> She doesn't say much unless you prompt her a lot. Things just appear to glide off her sometimes, and she doesn't seem to absorb or show much feeling, not even when I've asked her to tell me what it felt like to come to this country, or to leave her family. But you know, she has these constantly re-occurring headaches, stomach aches and is enuretic sometimes. Though her room is clean and well maintained at the foster parents' house, it can really smell bad. And I've thought that her body seems to be communicating something different to what she's outwardly saying.

Meera told the story of Lily's relationship with her father that had endured despite many years of separation. The father, a civil servant in the homeland, had decided to flee to a neighbouring country as the civil war increased in intensity, but had returned when it was safe. Social Services had been able to establish contact temporarily with him during the early stages of Lily being in care, but he had disappeared for two years. Then, unexpectedly, Lily received a letter from him. She told Meera that she read it and that the contents had upset her because her father had told her that since she had left he had remarried, and that from this new marriage there were two children including a little girl. This new girl had been named Lily. At their next meeting Meera said

> I think she's feeling a lot of anger, resentment and hurt now because of that. The father had given a telephone number in his letter that Lily used to contact him. When she rang, the man on the other end of the telephone sounded different, not the voice that Lily had in her head from her childhood days. Also, Lily said, he sounded formal and cold, not like her 'real' dad, even when he called her by the pet name she was given in the family before leaving. Lily ended the telephone call, promising to ring back the following week, but she had not.

Meera reflected that

> It just raised all sorts of thoughts for me about separation and the ideas that the young people – they are now young people – have. They left a parent behind and this

is what Lily and I talked about. 'You were a child when you knew him, you had a certain relationship with him, perhaps that's what's fixed in your mind.' Now, she's very mature and she agreed with that. She said 'Yes, I remember him as a little girl, I remembered a different voice and I remembered something different.' But she still couldn't accept that there wasn't any warmth in the way he spoke to her.

Meera appeared to worry for Lily. She said she worked with the possibility that Lily would talk to her or to a therapist in a safe way about the knots of feelings that she held, and that the pace and timing of what to say to whom would need careful shepherding by Lily, and those who cared for her. Meera said she had deliberately changed the focus of work on becoming Lily's social worker 'from socialisation to reflection'. Lily had been fond of the previous social worker who had been concrete and practical, coordinating solicitors, doctors and teachers who had formed a protective part of the formal network that Lily experienced as safe. But now that these pegs were in place, and Lily had achieved Indefinite Leave to Remain in the United Kingdom, Meera sensed that Lily could bear to look back more easily than she had done in the first few years after arrival. So Meera showed within the interview her own capacity to be reflective and to understand the depth and dimension of some of Lily's experiences. She appeared to be sufficiently emotionally robust to receive some of the complex intensity Lily had to offer. She said that she found Lily engaging and hoped that the moments of talking about her feelings would, like pools of light, spread out and join up over time.

Althea's story of solidarity and hope

One of the recurrent features of the stories told by social workers was related to the need they saw for unaccompanied minors to re-establish an ordinary, and in some respects, an unremarkable life. In doing so the children wanted to unwrap themselves from the 'asylum seeker' cover, and move towards universal goals and hopes of academic and material success over time. Althea was one of the social workers who illustrated her willingness to help them unravel narrow labels and to define different dimensions of their identities as they re-gathered a thick, multi-layered life. She told the story of Bertha, a young woman aged 20 who was at university studying to be a midwife. Bertha had arrived in the United Kingdom four years ago after surviving many dangers. Althea had been her social worker throughout, picking her up at the port of entry and taking her to her first placement in a children's home.

> I arrived [at the port of entry] and Bertha was huddling in the corner of the room with a blanket around her, shivering. She didn't even know where she was. I said you're in a place called England and nobody's going to take you away. You're safe, you are safe. I saw she was ill so I took her to our local hospital at 8 PM that evening. They did blood tests and confirmed she had malaria so she had to stay in. At about

2 o'clock in the morning I said, I've got to go, but you're going to be all right. This is a hospital. And she was just so exhausted she almost collapsed with exhaustion. She just flaked out, literally flaked out.

Althea said that Bertha had trusted her from the outset and had talked to her openly about her childhood, as well as her suffering during the course of forced migration from her country. Althea knew, from other experiences of working with unaccompanied minors, of children who would take years to tell their 'true' stories. Yet Bertha's story, raw and visible from the beginning, made Althea feel wretched, compelled to listen, flooded with distress and determined not to abandon her. The high emotional contact between them turned, over the years that they knew each other, into a broad and affectionate relationship.

Bertha was the younger of two children. Her older brother and she grew up in a family that Bertha described as happy. Bertha loved her brother and felt protected by him. When she was 13-years of age, civil war broke out in her country of origin. The family was displaced for a number of years, seeking shelter from one town to another as warring factions fought for military and political control within their country. Then, Althea explained

> Four years ago, the rebels were working their way up the country and they came to the town [where the family was sheltering]. It was during the night time, and the soldiers went into the house and beat up her father. The brother went to help and the soldiers killed him, they shot him in the neck and then they beat her father to death. Bertha described it very vividly and her mother said to her run and they both left from the back of the house and ran. As she ran she said they were shooting at her and she could hear the bullets flying past her. And then she stopped and they stabbed her in her shoulder and her arm. Three of the soldiers raped her, but did not kill her. She has asked me if I could help her get rid of these scars and although we took her to the hospital, it's difficult to hide these wounds because when she sees them it reminds her. And she was raped several more times before she made it to this country. So her story is dreadful.

Bertha lost all contact with her mother, and though she hoped that her brother had survived the shooting, she also knew that it was unlikely that he had. She continued to find life difficult in many respects. After moving to the children's home, she became pregnant through one of the other residents, also an asylum seeker. She had a termination that Althea supported her through. With Althea's help, Bertha moved on to self-contained accommodation, and gradually began to establish a rhythm and pattern to her daily life. She took great care in her appearance, dressing neatly and with flair. Her flat was sometimes untidy, but when she went out, 'there's not a hair out of place, she looks absolutely gorgeous'. She enrolled at a local college for English classes, and eventually took a Diploma in Health and Social Care, earning good grades that allowed her entry to University. She considered the daily routine of education a balm, and found an escape in academic progression and achievement that she could not find in other aspects of life. She told Althea that she experienced recurrent nightmares, broken sleep, lack of concentration and a pervasive lethargy that she found hard to dissolve. When Bertha was late with her assignments, Althea would ensure that tutors understood both the reasons for non-submission, as well as Bertha's will to succeed.

> I met one of the tutors when Bertha had about a week off, and I said to her does your tutor know anything about what has happened to you? And she said no. I said do you think it would help if she knew some, not all, whatever you want to share with her, and I'll be with you while you do that. And she shared some of the experiences about the rape, which was good because then they were really, really supportive, so if she was late with an assignment or something, the encouragement was there and they understood.

Althea said that over time Bertha had learnt that she could be 'bossy' and fierce with her in a familial way without altering Althea's commitment to her well-being. Differences of view were contested robustly, and resolved with an open expression of positive regard. Bertha had found ingredients that allowed her to cook food from the homeland, and Althea recognised how powerful the need was for Bertha both to eat 'home food' and to provide for others as she did so.

> I went round once and was picking her up to take her to the group [for unaccompanied minors] and she'd just cooked chicken and rice. I said it really smells nice. She insisted I have some. So I had this little bowl of rice and this chicken. It was as tough as old boots and it was so spicy. She said 'that's a proper chicken from [my country]'. And I ended up fighting with this chicken leg, and I managed to eat some of it. I said why is it so tough? She said that's because it needs to last me a few days. Cook it up properly. Never get any tummy problems or anything, but I said an old chicken like this – maybe it walked all the way here from [your country]. It was just unbelievable. We laughed.

Together Althea and Bertha had built up friendships for her from people in the community of origin whom she felt safe with, particularly women who were themselves asylum seekers. They had attended weddings together from within this network. Bertha had turned to Althea to protect her from men that she felt were approaching her on these social occasions. The ferocity of fear that emerged in Bertha when she felt the heat of unwanted attention made Althea feel as if she was acting in place of her mother, particularly when Bertha could not use her own strength to her advantage:

> I don't know whether it is about the rapes and what's happened to her, she just hasn't got that strength to be powerful within a relationship. And I think she would be taken advantage of because, like I said, she shouts and bawls and we shout at each other, but she wasn't actually able to say go away, I'm not interested.

So Althea worried for her, backed her up, and thought about her future and whether any good could come from such brutal disruptions in her life. Overall, Althea was not able to summon a clear prognosis. For example, she felt that there was something understandable about the wish to become a midwife, but also something misunderstood – and that Bertha needed much more time to understand her losses in order to focus more clearly on the gains. But Althea was clear that she did not see Bertha as a tragic victim, and in some respects the will to survive meant that Bertha would be hopeful and vocal in the world

> She wants to succeed, she wants to do well here, wants to have a good job. She and I often said this can either ruin your life for ever or it's not going to, and it's in our hand here. Let's work forward. And I think she very much believes that it's not going to finish her life forever. And I think it's almost like 'my mum and dad would have been proud of me if they could see me now'. Because I was saying, I'm very proud of you and your mum and dad would be so proud of you. She's not a victim. She is a survivor. I think that is very important that you're a survivor in all this.

Althea said that she hoped to be at Bertha's wedding one day. In the meantime, the two of them maintained regular telephone contact, with occasional social activities merging with the more formal review events.

Reflecting on the stories

Looking back at the three main questions that I had asked the social workers, the stories told by David, Meera and Althea came to signify a number of things to me about the ways contemporary practice with unaccompanied minors could be both complex and demanding. None of the characters had a 'neat' story to tell from which a template of effective practice could be shaped. They were diverse and connected, and it was these similarities and differences that interested me.

David's story confirmed that he knew very little about Leo's life. The ebb and flow of the work suggested that the relationship was experienced by him as thin, contorted by major forces beyond his control. The absence of clarity about the past and the future coincided to create a cluster of dissatisfactions. David's story also contained elements of lack of self-esteem, suspicion, and a sense of hopeless engagement which appeared to occlude his sight of providing practical help that Leo – like many of refugee children – would almost certainly have found useful in bedding down in the new country. Looking at David's story from some perspectives could have presented him as a functionary, a hostile border guard, or as someone focused on surface issues and lacking dimension and depth in his work. Indeed David's own account of disaffection and remoteness could have added to the broader views of social workers skidding past vulnerability to create and sustain ineffective practice.

Yet within this wrapping of 'remote control', there were specks of hope. David provided regular contact, appeared to be reliable, and act as an advocate at times. Key players from the formal network – lawyer, teacher, doctor, and carer – were arranged around Leo to assist with the practicalities of resettlement. Even though he felt suspicious about Leo's silence and barred from entry to parts of Leo's life, this practical focus of his work, allied to his willingness to reflect on what he did not know and to entertain uncertainty, suggested to me that David and Leo had reached not so much an impasse as an equilibrium of sorts, shaped by their own preferences and needs, as well as the contextual constraints that they faced.

Meera had chosen, perhaps because of the way her own way of working latched on to Lily's perceived needs, to try and unlock some of Lily's past. Lily's natural circumspection and the turbulent emotional world it covered were aspects that Meera saw, and resettlement meant creating a frame of emotionality that would allow Lily to see her life in some sort of focus. In comparison to David creating local maps that worked, Meera attempted to be a cartographer who mapped Lily's territory of feelings. With this broadly therapeutic intent, the connections between roots and shoots were kept alive, but in some respects in ways that were evocative and unmanageable for Lily at times. So one of the potential critiques of Meera's approach could have been to view it as an uninvited intrusion, with a remembrance of things past bringing home loss, and an acute sense of displacement. Yet as Blackwell (1997) observes in reference to therapeutic work with refugees, Meera was also able to witness some of Lily's distress, and to absorb some of the emotional impact on Lily of her father's remoteness. In doing so, part of her day-to-day practice appeared to use her capacity to be still, honest, kind and emotionally robust, so that Lily could look back at the texture and pattern of her life, and in understanding it more clearly, perhaps look forward with greater equanimity.

For Bertha, meeting Althea appeared to have been a salvation. Bertha's story spilled out quickly because she could not carry its weight and momentum alone. The structure of a trusting relationship, where Althea emphasised safety, began to be established at first encounter, and there was a clear sense in the interview with Althea that she had needed to rescue Bertha. As the interview progressed, and Althea described the layers of commitment she had made to Bertha, her capacity to fight for resources, to plan a future for Bertha and to be relentlessly optimistic distilled Parton and O'Byrne's (2000) reference to 'constructive social work' as a practical-moral activity, dwelling in possibility despite the high gloom of the past, and the challenges of finding a safe path in the present and future. Here Althea laid out an image of herself as being a beacon of hope for Bertha in a way that allowed Bertha to feel like a protagonist rather than a victim of circumstance, a subversion of the suffering she had endured. The two of them, in a robust and companionable way were presented as survivors. Althea came as close as any of the social workers I interviewed to suggesting that she felt like a family member, perhaps a parent, for the unaccompanied minor. She was clear about her impact on Bertha's life, as well as the diffuse and durable commitment that she had made to ongoing contact. She saw the organic growth in the relationship as part of a broader professional responsibility, unconstrained by narrower definitions of professional accountability. Over time Althea became the '*single, human, recognisable face to the world*' (Utting, 2003) that Bertha wanted her to be, a champion for Bertha's safety, well-being and success.

In all, the absence of neatness in the stories tells a story in itself. The social workers showed overall that they could listen to and tell thick stories about the children, even when the children themselves were committed to keeping silent. Similarly, in listening to the social workers, I realised that as a researcher I had a choice about how I represented their stories, and that I could look at them beyond the 'evaluating effective practice' frame. The social workers' thicker stories were ones where they said that they tried to deal with the capricious events that had propelled unaccompanied minors into their paths by being consistent and practically helpful, therapeutically minded and companionable. But this sometimes happened in quite rough and ready ways. In my mind, it is this roughness and the lack of definition about contemporary social work practice, that mirrors a broader debate about who is rough and who is neat, who we shelter as worthwhile, and who we keep on the borders of respectability and citizenship. Social work by its nature is a rough profession, working with refugee children on the margins of belonging. Neither is likely to move fluently towards acclaim, and both are liable to be represented and evaluated in thin ways. But these rough, thick stories also show that together, where there is a commitment to help there is hope, and that without the comfort of 'best practice guidelines' people do the best they can in the circumstances they find themselves in, whether their actions are small or large, invisible or bold.

References

Bertrand, D. (2000). The autobiographical method of investigating the psychosocial wellness of refugees. In F. L. Ahern (ed.), *Psychosocial Wellness of Refugees. Issues of Qualitative and Quantitative Research*. New York: Berghahn Books.

Blackwell, D. (1997). Holding, containing and bearing witness: the problem of helpfulness in encounters with torture survivors, *Journal of Social Work Practice*, 11 (2): 81–89.

Bracken, P. J. and Petty, C. (1998). *Rethinking the Trauma of War*. London: Save the Children.

Daniel, E. V. and Knudson, J. C. (1995). *Mistrusting Refugees*. London: University of California Press.

Dingwall, R. (1980). Ethics and ethnography, *Sociological Review*, 8 (4): 871–891.

Ferguson, H. (2003). Outline of a critical best practice perspective on social work and social care, *British Journal of Social Work*, 33: 1005–1024.

Geertz, C. (1973). *The Interpretation of Cultures*. New York, Basic Books.

Humphries, B. (2004). An unacceptable role for social work: implementing immigration policy, *British Journal of Social Work* 34 (1): 93–107.

Hynes, T. (2003). *The Issue of 'Trust' and 'Mistrust' in Research with Refugees: Choices, Caveats and Considerations for Researchers.* Geneva: UNHCR Evaluation and Policy Analysis Unit.

Jacobson, K. and Landau, L. (2003). *Researching Refugees: Some Methodological and Ethical Considerations in Social Science and Forced Migration.* Geneva: UNHCR Evaluation and Policy Unit.

Kohli, R. K. S. (2007). *Social Work with Unaccompanied Asylum Seeking Children.* (Basingstoke: Palgrave Macmillan).

LeCroy, C. W. (2002). *The Call to Social Work: Life Stories.* California: Sage.

Lee, R. M. (1993). *Doing Research on Sensitive Topics.* London: Sage.

Parton, N. and O'Byrne, P. (2000). *Constructive Social Work: Towards a New Practice.* Basingstoke: Palgrave MacMillan.

Robinson, V. and Segrott, J. (2002). *Understanding the Decision-Making of Asylum Seekers,* Finding 172. London: Home Office Research, Development and Statistics Directorate.

Seale, C. (1999). *The Quality of Qualitative Research.* (London: Sage)

Spencer, L., Ritchie, J., Lewis, J. and Dillon, L. (2003). *Quality in Qualitative Evaluation: A Framework for Assessing Research Evidence.* London: Cabinet Office.

Stanley, K. (2001). *Cold Comfort. Young Separated Refugees in England.* London: Save the Children.

Utting, W. (2003). The role of the child's social worker. In K. Bilton, *Be My Social Worker: The Role of the Child's Social Worker.* Birmingham: British Association for Social Workers/Venture Press.

CHAPTER 4

Assessment Practice with Unaccompanied Children: Exploring Exceptions to the Problem

Fiona Mitchell

Introduction

This chapter focuses upon needs assessment practice with unaccompanied asylum seeking children who have arrived into England. There are three things common to the exiled lives of unaccompanied children. They are separated from their parents or customary care givers, they are cut off from their country of origin and they are subject to immigration controls. A range of needs is likely to arise from these quite exceptional circumstances; their past experiences may also represent risk factors for children and young people in their present and future lives. It is for these reasons that unaccompanied children become the responsibility of local authority social services departments in England. The local authority is required to meet their needs and to find ways to mediate the levels of risk that these children and young people are exposed to. The events precipitating their current circumstances and the way in which individual children and young people have experienced and continue to experience them is likely to differ. Therefore, an ongoing process of assessment is necessary to build an in-depth understanding of the vulnerabilities and competencies of each child or young person, to appreciate the risk and protective factors resulting from their circumstances, and to plan service responses appropriate to their needs and wishes.

Research studies have indicated that there has been considerable variability in the occurrence of needs assessments, in the procedures that are employed and in the overall quality of assessments within and between local authorities in England (Munoz, 1999; Stanley, 2001; Children's Legal Centre, 2003). For example, the Audit Commission (2000) suggested, 'many authorities, for example, do not offer 16 and 17 year old unaccompanied children a full needs assessment' (66). Stone (2000) reported that almost three-quarters of the 54 local authorities surveyed were not assessing the needs of unaccompanied children with reference to the recently introduced national statutory guidance on assessment. Studies have also inferred from evidence about young people's later lives that needs assessment either may not have taken place, were ineffective or were not adequately implemented to meet the needs of these children and young people (Kidane, 2001a; Stanley, 2001; Dennis, 2002). These studies have provided limited data on the incidence rate of assessments or on the nature of the assessments that take place. This, therefore, became a research aim of a recent study that explored the response of social services departments to the needs of unaccompanied children (Wade et al., 2005). Based on an analysis of social work case records, this study identified that assessments often did take place but that they were frequently of poor quality – initial assessments took place in 88 per cent of the 212 cases surveyed but 68 per cent of those cases were rated as having an assessment that was 'less than adequate' (see the following section).

Following Parton and O'Byrne (2000), who explore social constructionist approaches for social work practice, this chapter takes as a springboard the idea that 'what the problem *is not*, or what is happening when the problem is not, leads us to exceptions to the problem, and these exceptions help us to see possibilities for change' (56). The 'problem' that we are concerned with in this chapter is the occurrence of poor quality needs assessments of unaccompanied children referred to social services departments. In this chapter, we aim to focus on the exceptions to the 'problem' – which in the context of this study's research findings is the 32 per cent of cases that were classified as having an assessment that was 'adequate or better'. By doing so, it is hoped that the chapter will help to illuminate possibilities for change.

The research study and its findings on needs assessment

The study reported on in this chapter was an exploratory one that focused upon the response of social services departments to referrals of unaccompanied children. It took place in three local authorities in England; these included a London borough, a county in the South and a city in the North. Together, the participating authorities represented a range of different contexts in which services were delivered at the time of the study. A sample of cases was selected from all new referrals to the three authorities within an 18-month period (running from 1 March 2001 to 31 August 2002). The sample was randomly selected but stratified to include cases of both boys and girls, those under and over 16, and cases that were referred within and beyond the past nine months. This was to ensure that the sample contained a range of cases, including some who were referred more recently and some who had been supported for some time. In the end, data was collected from social work records on cases that concerned a

Table 4.1   Overview of the Research
Methodology and Sample

Data source	Number of cases in sample			
	LA 1	LA 2	LA 3	Total
Social work case records	72	72	68	212
Qualitative interviews with young people	10	9	12	31
Qualitative interviews with practitioners	9	7	12	28

total of 212 children and young people; additional data was collected for a smaller sub-sample of 31 young people through separate qualitative interviews conducted with them and the practitioners who were most familiar with their case. An overview of the sample is provided in Table 4.1.

With reference to assessment, the three data sources offered different things. The social work case files provided a record of the assessment. From this, it was possible to build a picture of the assessment process and content. For example, data was collected on who was involved in the assessment, when it was conducted, and on the areas of young people's lives that it covered. From the interviews with young people, it was possible to gain some insight into how they had experienced their first contacts with social services. From the interviews with practitioners, it was possible to explore factors that they felt had affected initial and ongoing assessment practice with unaccompanied children.

Building a picture of assessment practice

On the basis of the data collected from case records, it was possible to discern that in 88 per cent of cases an initial assessment had taken place. Cases were classified as having an initial assessment where there was evidence of a process or procedure where *some* assessment had been made in the days and weeks immediately following referral. This classification does not reflect the parameters, particularly the timescales, set by the guidance or the pro forma introduced by the 'Framework for Assessment of Children in Need and their Families' (assessment framework) (Department of Health, 2000 et al.), as the study predated its introduction. The classification also did not reflect any evaluation of the quality of the assessments that had taken place, and consequently, had limited relevance to building a picture of assessment practice. Therefore, a further stage of analysis was undertaken to rate the 'adequacy' of the initial assessments.

This involved the researchers drawing together a pen picture for each case to elucidate the main strengths and weaknesses of the assessment conducted, and making a judgement on its 'adequacy'. Assessments were coded as 'adequate or better' where there was evidence that a comprehensive needs assessment had been conducted *and* that an adequate plan to respond to any identified needs had been made. And as 'less than adequate' where the evidence available demonstrated a less than comprehensive assessment of need *and/or* a poor response to any needs identified. 68 per cent of cases were rated as 'less than adequate' and 32 per cent as 'adequate or better'. The measure is an approximate one but it was one that was consistently applied across the sample and for that reason has some validity. Rating the cases in this way allowed us to explore, both quantitatively and qualitatively, what distinguished them from each other.

Qualitatively, the patterns identified reflected what we understand, as documented by a wealth of practice literature and guidance, distinguishes good assessment practice from poor. Those coded as 'adequate or better' were timely. Information was gathered from and about the children and young people, and was clearly recorded. Evidence demonstrated that a *range* of developmental needs had been considered; due account was taken of possible or evident risks, and ways in which these could be mediated. There was also evidence of practitioners 'weighing up' this information, noting gaps in their knowledge and the potential implications, and formulating plans to meet the needs identified through a range of clearly defined actions. The actions taken or planned were immediate or short-term as well as in the long-term (such as the need to gather more information over time). In general, the converse characterised the cases coded as 'less than adequate'.

Quantitatively, further analysis revealed a number of patterns. Better quality assessments were more likely to have been carried out by qualified social workers ($p < 0.001$; $n = 166$); 59 per cent of assessments were conducted by social workers and were adequate or better compared with just 14 per cent of those conducted by unqualified practitioners. They were also more likely to be better if the assessments were undertaken in children's asylum teams ($p < 0.001$; $n = 212$); 79 per cent of those undertaken within children's teams were adequate or better compared with only 16 per cent of those undertaken within other teams, such as generic asylum teams or by agencies external to the social services departments. They were more likely to concern younger children than older young people ($p = < 0.001$; $n = 212$): 48 per cent of those who were under 16 at the point of referral received an assessment that was deemed to be adequate or better compared with 18 of those who were 16 or over.

Building an understanding of assessment practice

Analysis of the qualitative data collected in interviews with young people and practitioners revealed a difference in approaches to assessment. These can be understood with reference to the procedural and exchange models of assessment identified by Smale et al. (1993). Milner and O'Byrne (2002) describe these models and suggest that they are closely linked to the salience given by social workers to risk, resources or needs factors. With the procedural model, 'the social worker fulfils agency function by gathering information to see whether the subject fits the criteria for services. Little judgement is required, and it is likely that checklists will be used' (52). Whereas with the exchange model,

> all people are viewed as experts on their own problems, with an emphasis on exchanging information. The social workers follow or track what other people are saying rather than interpreting what they think is meant, seek to identify internal resources and potential, and consider how best to help service users mobilise their internal and external resources in order to reach goals defined by them on their terms. (53)

Among qualified social workers and all workers based within children's teams, there was a tendency to adopt what appeared to approximate an exchange model. Practitioners tended to work with children and young people to identify their needs and to assist them to work with or restore their own problem-solving potential. This was despite the many practical challenges that they reported, such as the limited availability of information about the young people or of appropriately skilled interpreters. It was a process, not an event, which extended beyond the point of initial referral. Young people's accounts suggested that their initial encounters of social services laid the foundations for an ongoing 'exchange'. They described feeling comforted and reassured by the sensitivity of the practitioners with whom they first came into contact: 'the way she talked to us was like a mother', 'they just talked calmly and listened to us calmly'. They remembered being given explanations of social services' role: 'they said we are here to care for you'; 'the interpreter told me they are looking after children and that they would find me a placement – somewhere to stay'. Some practitioners reported that they felt that they had been able to achieve trusting relationships with young people over time. They felt they were able to do that through providing some stability for young people, being consistent in their approaches and responses, refraining from delving too deep, too soon, being non-judgemental and taking care to inform young people of how they could and couldn't help.

This contrasted strikingly with the approach taken in asylum teams, where a procedural model appeared to predominate. The limitations of which are well illustrated by the following comment by one practitioner, 'the initial assessment is just straightforward – your name, got any money, any health issues – it is just a standard form for everyone on whether they would be accepted for a service'. In these contexts, it appeared that assessment practice seldom extended beyond a basic, eligibility screening process. Young people who had experienced these assessments felt that they had very few options available to them, and that they had had to 'fight' for the little support they had received. These experiences closed off any opportunities for exchange as illustrated by these young people's perspectives – 'what's the point in telling, they are not going to help you anyway' or 'I hated coming inside this office and asking them for something because I knew they would just not be helpful at all.'

In the context of assessment practice with unaccompanied children, practitioners felt real barriers to communication existed, with limited availability of appropriately skilled interpreters. The uncertainty and ambiguity that surrounded young people's accounts of their past lives and experiences, too, was perceived to be a barrier to building relationships and to assessment of need, particularly as it was often perceived to be the sole source of information. Often, practitioners experienced such accounts as limited, inconsistent and contradictory in their content. The interviews with practitioners reflected, sometimes unpalatable, doubts about young people's own accounts of their lives, but there was a noticeable difference in the ways in which some qualified and experienced practitioners reflected on their own theories and what these meant for their practice. Understandings and explanations were attributed to why a young person might not present their 'true' story and it was possible for practitioners' theories to co-exist with young people's accounts of their past and present lives, although they were conflicting in detail. One senior practitioner felt that the staff within her team had become, 'very skilled at saying "it's ok to have different stories, we know this – it's normal"'. Those who had more experience, and were reflective in their practice seemed more ready or able to live with this ambiguity and to mediate any harmful affects of their emotional relationship to it. It seems that having access to good supervision assisted them to do this. Where this did not occur, for example, where unqualified workers became preoccupied by the inconsistencies it appears that this created an atmosphere of suspicion and, from the point of view of other social workers within the same team, that this then further impaired young people's ability to build trust.

Some felt that not knowing limited their ability to respond: 'we are dealing with unknown quantities, all of the time, we don't know about their background, we don't know what they've been through'. However, others talked about ways that they pieced together ideas about young people's family, socio-economic backgrounds and possible experiences. They formed views of young people's strengths and needs by drawing on their knowledge of child development and by taking account of their or others' observations of the young people in different contexts, such as in their placements, in educational classes, or, with their peers, over time. There was recognition that the passing of time was necessary and that it was not possible to build an in-depth picture of a young person's circumstances or experiences at the point of an initial referral. When working with unaccompanied children, it was felt that the time constraints set by the assessment framework (Department of Health, 2000 et al.) were not particularly realistic or appropriate for achieving an assessment on which to plan, even, short- to medium-term support. Ongoing assessment was crucial to informing short- to mid-term plans, as well as for needs that could be met in the longer-term. Stories shifted and changed over time and needs emerged as a result; one practitioner was emphatic in making the point 'it's about six months later when they have begun to feel safe that they actually begin to open up [and allow us to see] their emotional needs'.

What is happening when the problem is not?

The above summary of the study's research findings tells us something of what was happening within the context of three different local authorities. Assessment practice differed considerably. It appears that it often did consti-tute a 'problem' – overall, 68 per cent of cases included received an assessment that was less than adequate. Within our sample, 52 per cent of young people who were aged under 16 and 82 per cent of those aged 16 or over received an assessment that was less than adequate. It is possible to pursue this line of inquiry and construct an understanding of why this has happened. Answers may lie in the (mis)use or (mis)interpretation of the Children Act 1989 (Dennis, 2002; Stanley, 2001), in the differential levels of funding available to local authorities and their inability or reluctance to supplement these (Stanley, 2001; Free, 2005), in the hardening of attitudes and practices towards asylum seekers (Ayotte and Williamson, 2001) or in wider trends in relation to assess-ment practice, which historically have been found to be narrowly focused on risk (Department of Health, 1995b). But, the aim of this chapter is to under-stand what is happening when the problem is not. It is clear that social work practitioners – whether qualified or unqualified, field or managerial, experi-enced or inexperienced – are working within contexts that are constrained by, among others, legal duties, bureaucratic systems and available resources. These are facts of daily life for practitioners. Yet, it is also clear that there are instances when practitioners have got beyond these. Perhaps, there is some-thing to be learned from these exceptions; as Parton and O'Byrne (2000) say '[e]xceptions can then be those occasions when a little bit of the solution is already happening' (70). They counsel – to understand exceptions:

> The worker is simply curious about when things were better, how that happened, and especially what the person was doing differently made that possible. 'How did you do that?' is a key question therefore, key in two important respects: firstly in that the 'how' tells us about person's abilities; but, secondly, because if we emphasise the 'do' we are developing or enhancing the person's agency. If the question can prompt a person to figure out how he or she copes better sometimes, for example, then the person is empowered to repeat that behaviour more readily next time. (67)

In transferring these ideas to the context of my relationship to the above research findings on assessment, I might then develop a stronger curiosity about *when* assessments were better, about *how* it seems to have happened and about *what* it was that those who conducted good assessments were doing differently.

The research findings tell us about *when* things were better. It was when qualified social workers were involved, or assessments occurred within the context of a children's team or where younger children's needs were being assessed. Taking this a step further, the following patterns emerge:

- Qualified social workers were more likely to conduct better quality assessments. But unqualified workers working in children's teams were also more likely to conduct better quality assessments, than other unqualified workers.
- Better quality assessments were more likely to have occurred in children's teams. But better quality assessments were also more likely to occur in asylum teams when they were conducted by qualified social workers.
- Younger children were more likely to receive a better quality assessment. But older children also received better quality assessments when they were assessed by children's teams or by qualified workers.

The findings also tell us a little of *what* practitioners were doing differently. The social work case files demonstrated a process of gathering, recording and analysing information that evaluated a range of possible needs and informed plans to address those needs. The interview data demonstrated that where assessments worked well this process occurred in partnership with young people, and was founded upon trusting relationships that grew from communications that were respectful, kind and caring, and clear. This appeared to have been assisted by practitioners' willingness and capacity to reflect on their own experiences of direct work with young people and of the structural constraints that limited their work.

But, the question of *how* they managed to do it remains open to interpretation. The following discussion contains my own *reflections* on this question, informed by an exploration of the literature on assessment practice, my experience of working within the teams during the course of the data collection and of working on the data analysis.

Understanding how good assessment practice occurs

The following discussion presents an argument that is perhaps an obvious one, but it is perhaps also one that we have lost sight of in the context of research findings on the provision of services to unaccompanied children, particularly in relation to assessment where a considerable amount of energy has been expended upon highlighting the lack of implementation of legislative duty. Assessment in child and family social work is a complex task. There is a wealth of practice literature that explores the processes involved, the models and approaches that can be taken, and the extensive knowledge base that can be drawn on to inform analyses and judgements (Smale et al., 1993; Milner and O'Byrne, 2002; Walker and Beckett, 2003; Holland, 2004). Good assessment practice requires skill and knowledge, and the application of these has to be informed and mediated by the principles that underpin social work practice. Coulshed and Orme (2006) emphasise that 'in the current climate, where the organisation and delivery of social work services is changing and developing, it is the assessment process which is the one area of social work that depends on the skills, knowledge and values of those who have been educated and trained as social workers' (23). Given that good assessment practice in the study discussed above was linked to being trained and educated as a social worker, or to teams where their presence was in a majority, I want to explore this assertion further. So, what is it about the assessment task, in particular, that Coulshed and Orme (2006) consider is dependent upon someone participating in and completing a social work programme of education and training?

The assessment process involves identifying, gathering, analysing and understanding information. Integral to every stage is a practitioner's communication and analytical skills, as it is these that will determine their ability to elicit and make sense of information. This can also be understood as 'core skills' of communication, observation, reflection and evaluation (Couldshed and Orme, 2006). The gathering of information is dependent upon a practitioner's ability to engender trust and a rapport with people. '[B]eing punctual, reliable, courteous, friendly, honest and open' are attributes that have been identified as core skills of successful assessment work (Milner and O'Byrne, 2002: 24). The same authors draw attention to the findings of national government consultation with young people in care, which include 'listening, being non-judgemental, having a sense of humour, straight talking, and being trust worthy as essential elements of good professional practice' (24). These are key to an individual's experience of assessment and will affect their level of engagement and involvement in the process, whatever model of assessment is used. Being analytical means being capable of or given to analysing, to analyse is 'to examine in detail in order to discover meaning, essential features, etc' (Collins English Dictionary: 53). It is a skill that research has found that practitioners have struggled with (Cleaver, 2002; Cleaver and Walker, 2004), and for which guidance has been found to be lacking (Milner and O'Byrne, 2002; Holland, 2004).

With reference to this latter point, Milner and O'Byrne (2002) guide readers to adopt the same methodological rigour as sound qualitative research ...

[with] a clear statement of intent, which also demonstrates how one can be held accountable for one's values; a systematic approach to data collection from an identified range of sources, which is carefully checked for authenticity and which identifies gaps in information; the development of more than one hypothesis about the nature of the problems and solutions and a clear statement on how the final judgement can be tested in terms of demonstrable outcomes (60).

They emphasise the 'acid test of the assessment is the satisfaction with subsequent decisions and actions on the part of service users (empowerment in practice) and service providers'. In facilitating an assessment, social workers are likely to draw on a knowledge base informed by their awareness of social and psychological theory and research, their own practice experience and the legal framework. These will have a bearing on what information they decide to gather, the meaning they attribute to it in their analyses and the choices they make in planning for interventions. The practice guidance for the assessment framework cites the following quote in its introduction on knowledge:

> Social workers need a framework for understanding and helping children and families which takes into account the inner world of the self and the outer world of the environment, both in terms of relationships and in terms of the practicalities such as housing. It is the capacity of social workers to be aware of and integrate in their practice these different areas of concern, which defines the distinctive nature of their professional identity. (Schofield, 1998 cited in Department of Health, 2000: 4)

Opportunities for reflection with other colleagues and supervision with experienced colleagues can aid the process – some might say are essential to it (Walker and Beckett, 2003).

In the context of the above research study's findings, it is perhaps unsurprising then that it is those who have had the opportunity to develop their skills, to reflect upon and explore the relationship between values and practice, and develop their own knowledge base are more likely to conduct better assessments. However, their ability to do so seems to have been reinforced where they are working within children's teams – this also seems to have had a bearing on the practice of unqualified workers. In my experience, these teams offered an environment in which there is a common sense of purpose and values, and a culture that promoted reflection and the sharing of knowledge and perspectives. It is this that I feel helps us to understand *how* good quality assessments with unaccompanied children did occur and can improve.

There was a difference in the skill set, knowledge and values at play within the different types of teams, as well as in the opportunities that colleagues had to draw on each other's strengths and experience. In each of the three local authorities, there were, what we have described as, children's teams, specialist asylum teams that were child-centred or child-focused in their work. In these, the team leader was always an experienced, qualified social worker, and in two of the participating authorities, very closely involved in practice. Each of these teams also had at least one senior practitioner who was experienced and qualified, who was involved in supporting and supervising team members. In all three authorities, qualified social workers were in the majority in these teams; these workers were either newly qualified or had some experience, occasionally extensive, of working in a range of different areas of child and family social work (such as child and adolescent mental health, child protection, disability or generic children's service teams). There were fewer conflicting perspectives within these teams and it appears that this and the professional background of its members allowed for a more coherent value base within the teams. There appeared to be a stronger sense of solidarity amongst the staff within these teams; some explained that this was a product of their experience of establishing and developing a team together. This was strengthened further, in two of the authorities, by the view that the team leaders or the existence of the teams represented a stand against an apparent lack of corporate responsibility for or commitment to unaccompanied children. This contrasted with the other generic asylum teams or teams operating external to social services departments. Some of these were led by qualified senior social workers with the core staff formed by support workers, who appeared to have a limited knowledge of the legal and policy framework relevant to children and young people and of child development.

There was a palpable difference in the culture of the children's teams compared with the other generic asylum teams or teams operating external to the social services departments. The practitioners within the former were more inclined to reflect on and consider their practice and the impact it might have on children and young people's lives. This was evident in the day-to-day musings and interactions that I observed within all types of teams and in the perspectives taken by practitioners who were interviewed in relation to one of their cases. Their reference points were, what we understand and accept as, basic social work principles; such as those encapsulated in the definition provided by the British Association of Social Workers: 'social work should promote respect for human dignity and pursue social justice, through service to humanity, integrity and competence' (BASW, 2002: 2).

The qualified and unqualified social workers working within children's teams, and the qualified social workers working within other types of teams, also exhibited an awareness of the Children Act 1989. This may seem an obvious point, however, it was clear that there was some confusion in all of the teams about the rights and entitlements of unaccompanied minors. This confusion was connected to what were recent changes in welfare entitlements for single adults and families seeking asylum. However, for qualified workers within children's teams, despite, and perhaps in spite of, any nuances in entitlement that they came across, the principle of the 'best interests' of the child held steadfast as a point of reference. This led them to question the compromises that were made due to pressure of large caseloads, staff shortages and limited resources. In my mind, their reflections demonstrated a sense of agency that left them open to possibilities, and in some cases this led them to focus upon building relationships and assisting young people to mobilise their own inner resources to construct informal networks of support. Others, most often unqualified workers within generic teams, were more accepting of these restrictions, and for some, they did not even seem to represent compromises on the levels of support offered to young people.

Conclusion

In the context of assessment practice with unaccompanied children, the research findings discussed above do seem to reinforce the assertion made by Coulshed and Orme (2006) that good assessment practice is dependent upon the skills, values and knowledge of social workers. To reiterate, meaningful assessments can only occur if facilitated by professionals who are appropriately skilled, committed to basic social work principles, and able to draw on knowledge that will assist them and the children and young people that they are working to understand and deal with or overcome the problems that happen in their lives. Such professionals are those who have completed a programme of social work training and education and who are working within a context that promotes reflective practice and access to good supervision. They are also professionals who are able to maintain a connection to the principles and ethics that are laid down in the codes provided by associations of social work practitioners. Where assessment practice with unaccompanied children occurs within such a context, it is likely to vastly improve.

There are a number of resources available to practitioners who feel that they are operating in an unfamiliar context. The text produced by Milner and O'Bryne (2002) provides an in-depth exploration of many of the issues and themes that emerged in this analysis of assessment practice with unaccompanied children. Reflecting on these may assist practitioners to keep focused upon the basic fundamentals that underpin good assessment practice, while working within the context of the particular circumstances of unaccompanied children. Kidane (2001b), which supplements the Framework for the Assessment of Children in Need and their Families and was endorsed by the Department of Health, provides additional guidance for practitioners grappling with practice issues specific to unaccompanied children. The training pack that accompanied the original guidance to social services departments with regard to unaccompanied children (Department of Health, 1995a) collates a number of resources and provides valuable pointers for assessment practice and for working with interpreters.

References

Audit Commission. (2000). *Another Country: Implementing Dispersal under the Immigration and Asylum Act*. London: Audit Commission.

Ayotte, W. and Williamson, L. (2001). *Separated Children in the Uk: An Overview of the Current Situation*. London: Save the Children.

The Children's Legal Centre. (2003). *Mapping the Provision of Education and Social Services for Refugee and Asylum Seeker Children: Lessons from the Eastern Region*, Cambridge: The Children's Legal Centre.

BASW. (2002). *British Association of Social Workers Code of Ethics*. Birmingham: British Association of Social Workers.

Cleaver, H. (2002). Research findings informing the integrated children's system: the assessment framework. Paper presented at the DipSW and Child Care Programmes Conference, 20 March 2002, London.

Cleaver, H. and Walker, S. (2004). From policy to practice: the implementation of a new framework for social work assessments of children and families, *Child and Family Social Work*, 9: 81–90.

Coulshed, V. and Orme, J. (2006). *Social Work Practice*, 4th edn. Basingstoke: Palgrave MacMillan.

Dennis, J. (2002). *A Case for Change: How Refugee Children in England are Missing Out* London: The Children's Society, Save the Children, The Refugee Council.

Department of Health. (1995a). *Unaccompanied Asylum Seeking Children: A Practice Guide*. London: Department of Health.

——. (1995b). *Child Protection: Messages from Research*. London: HMSO.

——. (2000). *Assessing Children in Need and Their Families. Practice Guidance*. London: The Stationery Office.

Department of Health, Department for Education and Employment, and Home Office. (2000). *Framework for the Assessment of Children in Need and their Families*. London: The Stationery Office.

Free, E. (2005). *Local Authority Support to Unaccompanied Asylum Seeking Young People: Changes since the Hillingdon Judgement*. London: Save the Children.

Holland, S. (2004). *Child and Family Assessment in Social Work*. London: Sage.

Kidane, S. (2001a). *I Did Not Choose to Come Here: Listening to Refugee Children*. London: BAAF.

Kidane, S. (2001b). *Food, Shelter and Half a Chance: Assessing the Needs of Unaccompanied Asylum Seeking and Refugee Children*. London: BAAF.

Milner, J. and O' Byrne, P. (2002). *Assessment in Social Work*, 2nd edn. Basingstoke: Palgrave Macmillan.

Munoz, N. (1999). *Other People's Children: An Exploration of the Needs of and the Provision for 16- and 17-Year Old Unaccompanied Asylum Seekers*. London: Children of the Storm and London Guildhall University.

Parton, N. and O'Byrne, P. (2000). *Constructive Social Work: Towards a New Practice*. Basingstoke: Palgrave Macmillan.

Smale, G., Tuson, G., Biehal, N. and Marsh, P. (1993). *Empowerment, Assessment, Care Management and the Skilled Worker*. London: HMSO.

Stanley, K. (2001). *Cold Comfort: Young Separated Refugees in England*. London: Save the Children.

Stone, R. (2000). *Children First and Foremost: Meeting the Needs of Unaccompanied Asylum Seeking Children*. Barkingside: Barnardos.

Wade, J., Mitchell, F. and Baylis, G. (2005). *Unaccompanied Asylum Seeking Children. The Response of Social Work Services*. London: BAAF.

Walker, S. and Beckett, C. (2003). *Social Work Assessment and Intervention*. Lyme Regis: Russell House Publishing.

CHAPTER 5

Therapeutic Encounters between Young People, Bilingual Co-workers and Practitioners

Hitesh Raval

Introduction

This chapter first introduces some broad structural issues in relation to providing mental health service provision for young people who seek asylum or are refugees. It then considers their mental health needs through the lens of culturally competent therapeutic practice. The main focus of this chapter is the factors that practitioners may wish to consider when providing services for young people in the context of utilising language interpreters.

In their short lives many young people who seek political asylum have already been subject to violations or have witnessed the violation of others. A minority may also have taken part as child soldiers in the killing of others. A significant number of young people continue to remain at risk either in their country of origin or in their receiving country. They are likely to have endured threats to their personal safety and emotional well-being whilst undertaking perilous journeys before arriving at a destination of safety. Inevitably, reaching their destination is not the end of their journey, but only the beginning of new ones. Their transition continues in the host country with the search for physical and emotional sanctuary; one that relies on the support of unfamiliar people, and which occurs within an unpredictable and changing environment. They face new challenges arising out of bureaucratic asylum systems, prejudice and racism, and remain vulnerable to the impact that these may have on their psychological well-being.

It is a testament to their bravery and strength that many of these children and young people manage these enforced emotional life journeys alone. That they retain a level of optimism into their adulthood, whilst continuing to confront adversity in their lives, demonstrates the resilience that many of them posses. Whilst many young people make a very successful adaptation to their lives in a new country, they may also continue to confront unresolved painful issues. These issues are likely to have a greater impact where young people continue to be in a position of having limited power to change what is happening to them in their lives. For example, the hope of making a new life in the host country versus the pull to go back to the country of origin to find lost relatives, may create an irresolvable emotional conflict for the young person.

Service provision and training issues

Research confirms that host countries are often not well prepared nor sufficiently organised to respond to meeting the immediate practical and psychological needs of unaccompanied children and young people (Fazal and Stein, 2002; Hargreaves et al., 2003; Podgore et al., 2003). There is a significant lack of service provision for these young people aged 16 and 17 years (Myers, 2001). Dedicated services for this group of young people often tend to be patchy and located in the larger cities. The cultural sensitivity of services can be enhanced by having trained practitioners with similar cultural and linguistic backgrounds to those of the young people they help. Unfortunately, in the United Kingdom there are not many registered practitioners from similar community and cultural groups, as those of the young people served by health and social care services.

Young people also meet structural barriers to securing quality service provision due to factors such as the restrictions imposed on their citizen rights by virtue of the asylum seeking process in the United Kingdom. Being confined to detention centres, or being placed in parts of the United Kingdom where they have no natural networks with others from their home communities can increase the risk of emotional problems developing. Not knowing how to access health or social care, or having to confront inherent institutional attitudes or practices become further barriers to accessing professional help (Coker, 2001; Lamb and Smith, 2002; Carter, 2003; Shelton, 2003). Not being able to speak the main language of the host country becomes another significant barrier to accessing help. The availability of trained language interpreters, with substantive experience and knowledge about working in mental health settings, particularly for young people seeking refuge and asylum is varied across the United Kingdom.

Practitioner expertise in providing culturally competent and culturally sensitive services to these young people tends to vary across services and geographical locations. In the United Kingdom there continues to be a lack of adequate pre- and post-registration training specifically aimed at producing culturally competent health, mental health and social care practitioners (Patel et al., 2000; Raval, 2005). Training packages that enable practitioners to work effectively in meeting the broad range of needs of minority ethnic communities, including young people and children seeking asylum, are in the early stages of development.

The invaluable contribution of language interpreters and bilingual co-workers can often make an important difference in providing an effective service for young people. Yet, very few practitioners have had specific training in how to work profitably with language interpreters. Very few language interpreters have dedicated training in how to carry out their work in mental health settings. There remains a need in the United Kingdom for both types of training. In addition, joint training for practitioners and language interpreters is required if effective co-worker practice is to be developed. The predominant clinical literature to date is suggestive of practitioners making poor use of language interpreters (Gerrish, 2001; Lamb and Smith, 2002; Bischoff et al., 2003).

Though the provision of interpreting services in the United Kingdom is increasing, resources remain patchy across different regions, with variability in the level of experience and training undergone by interpreters particularly in relation to mental health. Many language interpreters continue to experience being marginalised, devalued and not being treated as professionals in their own right. They experience further marginalisation by virtue of belonging to minority ethnic groups. Many language interpreters are trained professionals in their own right but their academic or professional qualifications from their country of origin are often not recognised in the United Kingdom.

Understanding young people's responses to traumatic life events

Children and young people who have experienced violating life events and war tend to show elevated levels of psychological distress as measured by symptom checklists, and display physical complaints that are consistent with a response to trauma (Mckelvey and Webb, 1995; Qouta et al., 2005; Sourander, 1998; Hodes, 2000; Brune et al., 2002; Fazal and Stein, 2003; Hargreaves et al., 2003; Turner et al., 2003). However, some studies have not shown such elevated levels of distress in children when using symptom checklists (Wahlsten et al., 2002). Other authors have reported children to have lower self-esteem and less confidence in relation to their academic work (Loughry and Flouri, 2001; Slodnjak et al., 2002). The safety and welfare of children is placed at greater risk where they or their families experience higher levels of social exclusion, isolation, and deprivation (Jones and Kafetsios, 2002; Riddell-Heaney and Allott, 2003). Whilst, symptom checklists provide useful information about prevalence rates or general levels of distress, they may not be adequate for the purposes of clinical screening (Jones and Kafetsios, 2002). This type of research has also been criticised for its limitations in not being able to identify and explain the underlying psychological mechanisms leading to particular types of distress (Davey, 2003).

The prevalent model of understanding children and young people is that of trauma. Though this way of understanding young people is helpful, it is limiting where the sole focus of help remains specific to alleviating the emotional and behavioural symptoms associated with trauma. Negating the socio-political and cultural context in which the trauma has arisen and not finding solutions for the young person that tackle their broader needs places limits on the effectiveness of the practitioner's ability to help the young person.

Factors to consider when making a mental health assessment

Adverse life experiences and responses to them cannot simply be understood by focusing on the outward distress shown by the young person. A fuller assessment has to take account of the significance of past or current experiences on the young person, the circumstances that have led to their distress, their attempt to make some sense of these and their ability to narrate something of this at a given point in time (Smail, 1990; Rousseau et al., 1998; Gallagher et al., 2002; Bolea, et al., 2003; Whittaker et al., 2005). An understanding has to be developed about how the violence or oppression experienced by an individual has taken away facets of their social identity or their sense of 'home', and their internal and external resources to deal with the aftermath of these experiences (Papadopoulos, 2002 and 2003; Patel, 2003). Many young people forge new identities based on prevalent negative societal narratives about them within host communities and internalise these negative attributes as part of their being (Goffman, 1963).

Other important factors to consider include the ability of the adults to support the young person with his or her distress, how well the young person is adjusting to a new country, and what sense he or she has made of their traumatic experiences (Mekki-Berrada et al., 2001). It is also important to know about how long the young person has been living in a new country, the current hardships they are facing and the nature of their contact with relatives remaining in the country of origin. This kind of information is helpful when assessing what factors have the potential to serve a protective function for the young person and those that may increase the level of risk to their well-being (Rousseau, 1995; Papadopoulos, 2001; Fazal and Stein, 2002; Weine et al., 2003; Qouta et al., 2005). The stage of readiness of the young persons to explore their psychological distress, and the cultural appropriateness of the means by which to do this, are important to assess when planning what type of help to offer to them (Davies and Webb, 2000). The practitioner has to assess how ready the young person is to embark on psychological work.

The practitioner has to take account of the complex and inter-related circumstances that are impacting on a young person's emotional life. There may be the added complication of the legal process associated with seeking the right to remain in a country becoming intertwined with an assessment of the young person's mental health status (Tufnell, 2003). Practitioner have to give consideration to the impact of broader socio-political factors in making their clinical assessment and when deciding on what is likely to be the most therapeutic or helpful intervention to make at a given point in time. Helping the young persons identify useful organisations such as the International Red Cross may prove to be helpful in its own right if it helps them locate the whereabouts of close relatives. Perhaps only when the more immediate worries have been allayed will these young persons be in a position to make use of a psychosocial intervention aimed at looking at the underlying psychological distress that they have had to hold in abeyance.

Developing culturally competent ways of understanding and helping young people

Cultural competency incorporates issues relating to developing cultural and 'ethnic-specific' knowledge about specific ethnic groups, the awareness of and information about differences in religion and cultural attitudes towards health matters, as well as an examination of the attitudes that a health practitioner brings to their work. The model of cultural competence implies a coming together of personal competencies, organisational competence and service competence (Chandra, 1996). One such practitioner competency is being able to understand the psychological needs of the young person within his/her cultural context.

Another competency is being able to make effective use of language interpreters as they can support the practitioner in making a culturally competent assessment and in identifying a clinically sensitive intervention. The case for using a bilingual co-worker model between language interpreters and practitioners when carrying out clinical work has been made elsewhere (Raval, 2005; Raval and Maltby, 2005). This model of bilingual co-working is expanded on in this chapter in relation to carrying out therapeutic work with young people seeking asylum or living as refugees. Bilingual co-workers are a valuable resource for practitioners in carrying out their therapeutic work, and with the relevant training and experience bilingual co-workers can support this work more fully. An ability to draw on the skills of bilingual co-workers appropriately is an important cultural competency that practitioners need to possess.

The remainder of this chapter looks at drawing on this framework in carrying out clinical assessments and therapeutic work. Themes that are frequently encountered in clinical practice are drawn on in developing the key points and presenting some of the issues encountered in this work.

The importance of co-working and taking a structured approach

Effective practice utilising language interpreters needs to have the hallmarks of planning and structure. This structure needs to incorporate time for initial

planning, regular briefing and debriefing, and reflective practice for both the practitioner and the bilingual co-worker (Raval, 2005; Raval and Maltby, 2005).

The initial **planning** stage is crucial to developing an effective co-working relationship between the practitioner and bilingual co-worker. This serves a number of important functions. It first provides an opportunity for two people who have not worked with each other before to gain an understanding of each other's approach to their work. Language interpreters are unlikely to have had specific training in mental health or social care practice, and may not be familiar with the therapeutic framework or approach likely to be used by the practitioner. This time can be usefully spent by each worker familiarising themselves with each other's frameworks for practice.

The code of practice for language interpreters places emphasis on verbatim translation, which in many respects limits the way they can work. Even though this is the primary task, it is difficult for language interpreters to translate in a meaningful when they are unfamiliar with the jargon and rationale behind the way practitioners may choose to work. It is hard for an interpreter to support a mental health assessment when they are unfamiliar with mental health terminology or the intent behind the practitioner's questioning. Without mutual understanding it is difficult to develop trust and clarity about each others' roles (Raval, 1996, 2002, 2003; Raval and Smith, 2003). Mutual trust is vital for developing a good working relationship and creating a containing working relationship between the practitioner and the language interpreter, and between the two workers and the young person. The young person is unlikely to develop trust and a sense of being contained if they do not experience this between the practitioner and language interpreter.

Another important negotiation required in the planning stages is that of agreeing the remit and the role that a language interpreter is able to take on (Raval, 2003, 2005; Tribe and Raval, 2003). Where language interpreters are trained and experienced they are able to provide a broader supportive role in the work such as cultural consultancy, cultural brokerage, link working and advocacy. However, this should always be individually negotiated between the language interpreter and practitioner. As bilingual co-workers, interpreters can have a very helpful role in informing and educating the practitioner about cultural factors that may need to be kept in mind when carrying out a clinical assessment or ongoing therapeutic work. The bilingual co-worker can also be an immensely useful resource about current issues being faced by the young person in the immediate and local community.

Planning is also helpful in looking at mental health terminology and discussing culturally appropriate ways in which Western mental health constructs can be translated within the young person's frame of reference. A mutual understanding about terminology and the intent of the practitioner can make the task of the bilingual co-worker more manageable. There are times when the bilingual co-worker requires a longer conversation with the young person in order to elicit the information needed by the practitioner.

Ongoing **briefing** prior to seeing the young person can be used for updates and to plan the session. Informally, many language interpreters report that they are not given any information or background to the nature of the work, but expected to arrive on time for the appointment and go straight into the session with the practitioner. Being given no briefing places language interpreters at risk and undermines them in being able to carry out their work.

Debriefing after each session is also important to facilitate a dialogue about issues that may not have been possible to talk about in the presence of the young person. The nature and rationale of these short meetings need to be explained to the young person in order to maintain the trust. During the debriefing, the practitioner and bilingual co-worker can plan for further sessions with the young person, pick up on other issues coming up in the work, and explore with each other the emotional impact their work is having on them personally. This is particularly important if splits, distrust, and a lack of containment are to be avoided.

Reflective practice is now seen as integral to mental health professional trainings and through subsequent working life (Lavender, 2003). This is encouraged and supported in a number of ways including regular clinical supervision, management, and continuing professional development. Language interpreters are largely not supported in this way, though some specialised trauma and interpreting services are beginning to provide regular supervision or support groups for language interpreters. Debriefing with language interpreters can go to some extent in serving this function given the risk of vicarious trauma. Many language interpreters continue to carry the distressing emotional impact of the work on their own, and draw on individual coping strategies for managing this aspect of their work. However, if unresolved issues are not picked up on an ongoing basis they are likely to interfere with the therapeutic alliance or continuing work with the young person. As a worst case scenario the language interpreter might be so traumatised by the nature of mental health work or by the story they have heard from the young person, they may feel unable to continue with the work, or less willing to work in a mental health setting in the future. Many language interpreters also informally report that they feel unwanted or are treated disrespectfully by practitioners.

Carrying out clinical assessments using a co-working model

Young people bring a number of complex issues that they are facing in their daily lives. Therefore, no one theoretical model of clinical practice is sufficient if culturally sensitive and competent clinical assessments are to be carried out. A broader theoretical and contextual approach is required in order to understand the different levels of complexity often associated with a young person's life.

A fictitious amalgam case example will now be used to highlight the complexities that practitioners encounter, and as a means of illustration for how a clinical assessment, formulation and intervention might be carried out. The fictitious case material is presented as a continuous piece of work to suggest stages of work when certain assessment or intervention approaches might prove more useful than others. This way of illustration is used to highlight the different levels of understanding required to fully appreciate the multiple needs of the young person.

Yusuf's story

Yusuf a 17-year-old unaccompanied young person is referred by his social worker for post traumatic stress disorder (PTSD). Yusuf has complained of having nightmares and other PTSD-related symptoms. The referral contains very little history or other details of the support that Yusuf is currently receiving.

A planning meeting is arranged with a community language interpreter prior to meeting Yusuf. During this meeting it is agreed the language interpreter has other relevant work experience in order to take on cultural consultancy and advocacy tasks that are in keeping with the bilingual co-worker role. As a bilingual co-worker the language interpreter is helpful in informing the mental health practitioner about the cultural and local community context of other young people from the same country of origin as Yusuf. The practitioner is given information about how many young people are having difficulties adjusting to school and a new language, and how they are ostracised by peers from the host country. The bilingual co-worker and practitioner talk about their different levels of experiences in working with young people in similar predicaments to Yusuf, and inform each other about their respective ways of working which draw on very different models of understanding human distress.

At the initial meeting with Yusuf it transpires that his primary concerns are about not knowing the whereabouts of his family in his country of origin, and not having his legal status confirmed in the United Kingdom. He is also getting into fights at college. He is living in a bed and breakfast establishment. He talks about the onset of his nightmares and panic attacks six months earlier after watching a television programme about child soldiers in his country of origin. He is increasingly becoming distressed by his nightmares and shortness of breath, and he wants to be prescribed medication to alleviate these. In the first meeting Yusuf is reluctant to give much personal history and is not clear about why he is seeing a mental health practitioner.

From a systemic perspective it is possible to identify several contextual factors impacting on his life. He has limited finances to go out and knows very few people in the locality. He is desperate to make contact with his family but lacks the know-how about how to do this. Even if he were to establish contact he is worried that this might place him or his family at a greater risk to their safety. On subsequent appointments he talks more about his circumstances and re-defines his main distress as stemming from the uncertainty about his asylum claim. He perceives his life as being on hold until his asylum claim has been sorted out. His main worry is that of being sent back to his country of origin. This worry seems to feed into feelings of panic particularly when he is alone in his room.

Gradually through his narrative it becomes possible to locate his personal story in the context of societal and family narratives about him. He has a strong sense of him self as a survivor. This draws on a broader societal narrative from his country of origin of a people who have to live and survive in a harsh environmental and more recently a persecutory political climate. He is the son of a noble family line and being the eldest child of his parents has been the one who was chosen to escape persecution. As the eldest son he should be home to financially support his family. This responsibility carries a heavy weight in his heart, as does his wish to return home to redress the wrongs done to his people. His story contains a sense of pride, self-worth, and responsibility. In contrast, he is all too aware of the narratives that have currency in the host community of people like him. He is a burden to the state, an illegal entrant, a criminal, worthless and an unwanted refugee, which is often what he feels about himself.

The debriefing sessions prove helpful for the practitioner and bilingual co-worker to understand their emotional responses to the young person. The co-worker reflects on feeling guilty about having escaped and survived when many of his family and contemporaries were killed in his country of origin, and connects this with what the young person may be feeling. Working with this young person has brought him back in touch with his own traumatic experiences from the past and the struggles he faces being recognised for his abilities rather than as an unwanted foreigner in the United Kingdom. The female practitioner reflects on feeling guilty about how privileged a life she has in comparison, and her unease with her country's response to supporting young people seeking asylum or refuge. As a recently qualified young mental health practitioner she can also identify with Yusuf's sense of powerlessness. She feels that she has little power to make substantial change in the service provision for young people like Yusuf.

The approach to helping Yusuf is a collaborative one. Each individual perspective and insight into how best to understand what is happening is taken into account (Kaufert, 1990). Yusuf locates the main area for change as wanting to be granted asylum status and indefinite leave to remain, which he feels will go a long way to alleviate his psychological problems. The bilingual co-worker has a contextual understanding of Yusuf's lack of connectedness with his community. The practitioner offers her understanding based on psychological models of human distress. Somehow these different perspectives will need to be integrated if the three of them are to arrive at shared aims for the work.

Developing a client centred understanding

The first few sessions highlight how the preliminary meetings with Yusuf require an initial assessment that is able to take account of a number of different levels of complex issues that he has to confront. All these levels of complexity are required in the assessment in order to build up a preliminary understanding. Areas of his strengths are also explored as part of developing a broader understanding. Despite his difficulties he is quite resourceful. He has a strong integrated sense of himself and hopes to make the most of his education. He has good insight and is able to reflect on his life experiences with a level of maturity beyond his age. He is strongly motivated to make changes to his life.

Yusuf is angry with his solicitor for not having secured him the right to remain in the United Kingdom and being granted asylum status, but is fond of his social worker. He is also angry with one of his college tutors whilst being positive about another. His feelings are quite polarised with regards to the two tutors. In the therapy sessions he seems to be fluctuating between being dismissive of one of the workers and over idealising the other, and readily moving positions in relation to the practitioner and the bilingual co-worker. In the debriefing it is helpful for the two workers to discuss their emotional reactions when working with Yusuf. There is a danger that the two workers will become polarised in their work with him. Giving voice to their emotions helps them to process their emotional responses towards him, and be able to understand what it must be like for Yusuf on a day-to-day basis. This helps with appreciating the fluctuating sense of despair and hope that Yusuf is managing in his life, but which seem irreconcilable in his mind. At another level this split is also symbolic of the political divide in his country of origin where the hope arising out of a change in the political regime has changed to despair. Yusuf's hope and despair in relation to trying to build a life for himself in the United Kingdom, is also mirrored in the therapeutic work. Making a connection between why he might be experiencing such strong emotions provides a useful starting point in helping him to make some sense of what has been happening in his life.

Yusuf's initial presentation seems to be consistent with many PTSD features. His eagerness to rid himself of the symptoms is evident and though disappointed at not being prescribed medication is willing to consider a psychological approach. He is informed that he can seek a further consultation with his General Physician (GP) with regard to exploring a medical intervention for his symptoms.

A preliminary assessment using a cognitive-behavioural therapy (CBT) framework is helpful in identifying triggering thoughts and behaviour associated with his nightmares and panic attacks. These signs of distress are however located in an emotional state that is fluctuating between despair and hope, anger and mistrust, uncertainty and fear, some level of ambivalence in forming trusting relationships with others, and feeling unable to decide where his future lies. These emotions are understandable when taking the context of his life experiences into account.

His ongoing distress is located in and perpetuated by contextual factors such as having to encounter and negotiate his way through an unfamiliar legal system, lack of social contact, uncertainty about housing and negativity from the host community. His experience of the temporary and unpredictable nature of close relationships and life are borne out. The two workers reflect on what at first seems like an overwhelming task in thinking about where to start in helping Yusuf. However, each person's emerging insight is of value and taken together gives a fuller explanation that all can use in reaching a consensus of where to begin in bringing about change for Yusuf.

Places to start

All three parties agree that from a contextual perspective Yusuf would benefit from having some stability, structure and predictability to his day. Independent of the meetings with Yusuf, and with his consent, the practitioner and bilingual co-worker arrange meetings with his social worker to explore more permanent housing arrangements for Yusuf, and to identify networks from his community that Yusuf can be linked with. His social worker also agrees to go with Yusuf to the solicitor to ensure that Yusuf is getting the right level of support with regard to his asylum claim.

The practitioner and bilingual worker also arrange a meeting with Yusuf's college to explore what further support he can get there. In discussing the reasons behind Yusuf getting into fights, it transpires that Yusuf is being taunted by a particular group of students. Regular times are set with the two tutors he is in most contact with for him to talk about difficulties he is having at college. During this meeting it becomes apparent that the college is struggling with other similar incidents of bullying of young people seeking refuge, and the tutors are divided in two camps as how to best deal with this. This dichotomy is reflected back by the practitioner in relation to the polarisation that Yusuf experiences, and the college agrees that they need to develop a more coherent policy so that the students are clear about how such behaviour is to be managed in the future. Having a contextual understanding of the challenges facing the college and in understanding something of the unspoken process in the way they are trying to manage these proves helpful. The college also initiates a training day on mental health issues facing young people seeking asylum and refuge as a means to support staff and enhance the existing robust ways in which they already support young people with a high level of emotional and educational need.

Yusuf is aware of the changes taking place within the supports around him, and is beginning to make more use of local community networks. He is pleased with initiating and finding shared accommodation with contacts he has made in his community. His readiness to explore psychological ways of managing his distress is also evident in his meetings with the practitioner and bilingual co-worker. He is keen to employ suggested practical cognitive-behavioural strategies in helping him manage the onset and duration of his panic attacks. As the work develops Yusuf continues to find the CBT strategies to be useful in managing his panic attacks or when he finds it difficult to get to sleep due to worrying about having nightmares.

Although he is able to make good use of these strategies he reports that his nightmares are becoming more vivid and distressing. His nightmares have now become more vivid and resemble his actual life experiences from his country of origin. He states his wish to talk about the real life trauma that he has encountered. He begins to talk about events that he had witnessed but which he had put to the back of his mind. He is able to start piecing together aspects of his lived experience that he could not make sense of, or was too painful to talk about or which he had been forgotten.

He becomes very distressed in the sessions and the emotional impact of this is visible in the bilingual co-worker. At this point the debriefing sessions become integral to the work. Yusuf talking about his lived traumatic experiences resonates with the bilingual co-worker who is reconnected with his pain of losing his family and coming to the United Kingdom on his own. Understanding his emotional responses in relation to Yusuf is helpful for the bilingual co-worker to process his feelings. The debriefing provides a level of containment for the bilingual co-worker, which in turn is containing for Yusuf. The debriefing also allows the practitioner to explore her feelings in relation to understanding distress that is outside of her lived experience.

At this stage she finds it helpful to explore her approach to helping Yusuf and her feelings with regard to this work in her clinical supervision with a senior practitioner. Of greatest impact is her sense of despair and loss of hope about whether her work is 'good enough' in being able to help Yusuf. She is reminded in supervision of how Yusuf too has moved from points of hope to despair. What is important is that both the practitioner and bilingual co-worker are able to hold Yusuf's pain, bear witness to his story and validate his traumatic experiences, in a way that many others he has encountered have not.

Places to go

Through these sessions another theme that emerges is that of the actions of others not making any sense and the injustices in life. Yusuf's narrative seems both embedded in and a product of his lived experiences and encounters with others. Making sense of the unpredictability, helplessness, despair, strength, survival and hope that Yusuf experiences now become useful metaphors in the work. As Yusuf begins to make his own links and give meaning to what he has experienced in his life, these metaphors become useful anchors in the work. It becomes possible for him to distinguish aspects of his life where he has personal agency and those where he is subject to the agency of others, and to recognise the interplay between the two. He is able to identify his sense of agency, resourcefulness, quick thinking and strength when he had to escape his country of origin on his own. He is able to talk about socio-political systems that are outside of his control and which he perceives as unjust at times, though knowing that they are also there to support him. He appears to take more charge of his situation and becomes more proactive in making contact with his solicitor rather than waiting to be contacted.

He is also able to see how these attributes have been useful in adjusting to life in the United Kingdom such as using his own initiative in securing more permanent accommodation. At this stage he is also able to reconnect with other positive narratives of himself, which to date have remained dormant. Being reminded of other positive historical cultural narratives by the bilingual co-worker, these become useful points of connection. Yusuf also becomes more questioning of his acceptance of the negative societal narratives that he has encountered in the United Kingdom about refugees, and wishes to explore how these are impacting on his identity. He has a renewed sense of himself that seems to be allowing him to take risks in building up personal relationships. Though Yusuf is able to readjust his short-term plans, he remains wary of making any long-term plans, should he be sent back to his country of origin.

The college is helpful in supporting Yusuf with planning for his future educational needs and Yusuf is proactive in getting information about advanced courses he might do. His social worker has also been able to connect Yusuf with support agencies that may help him locate the whereabouts of his parents. There is regular review of the work with Yusuf that take account of his views, and the perspectives of the bilingual co-worker and practitioner. The aims of the sessions are regularly reviewed to ensure that Yusuf is able to indicate his needs at different points in time.

Summary

In summary, this chapter has tried to provide a framework for thinking about working with young people who have the additional need for language interpretation. A collaborative approach that integrates the personhood of the young person, bilingual co-worker and practitioner into the work is suggested. It is primarily our humanness that provides the relational and therapeutic point of connection. Given this, the model of language interpreting as one where the interpreter should be no more than a neutral conduit, completely negates the personhood of the interpreter and places restrictions on bringing about therapeutic change. To demote our humanness in favour of theoretical affiliation, therapeutic technique, or mode of understanding the human condition limits our ability to work with young people, and our ability to learn from them.

I have felt honoured and priviledged in having the opportunity of working with young people and bilingual co-workers. Their generosity in sharing their experiences and stories has enriched my understanding of their lives and my capacity to work in a more culturally competent manner.

References

Bischoff, A., Bovier, P. A., Isah, R., Françoise, G., Ariel, E. and Louis, L. (2003). Language barriers between nurses and asylum seekers: their impact on symptom reporting and referral, *Social Science and Medicine,* 57 (3): 503–512.

Bolea, P. S., Grant, G., Burgess, M., and Plasa, O. (2003). 'Trauma of children of the Sudan: a constructivist exploration'. *Child Welfare,* 82 (2): 219–233.

Brune, M., Haasen, C., Krausz, M., Yagdiran, O., Bustos, E., and Eisenman, D. (2002). Belief systems as coping factors for traumatised refugees: a pilot study, *European Psychiatry, The Journal of the Association of European Psychiatrists,* 17 (8): 451–458.

Carter, B. (2003). Think child, not refugee, *Journal of Child Health Care,* 7 (1): 4–6.

Chandra, J. (1996). *Facing up to Difference.* London: Kings Fund.

Coker, N. (2001). (ed.), *Racism in Medicine: An Agendaf For Change.* London: Kings Fund.

Davey, G. (2003). Doing clinical psychology research: what is interesting isn't always useful. *The Psychologist,* 16 (8): 412–416.

Davies, M. and Webb, E. (2000). Promoting the psychological well being of refugee children, *Clinical Child Psychology and Psychiatry,* 5 (4): 541–562.

Fazal, M. and Stein, A. (2002). The mental health of refugee children, *Archives of Disease in Childhood,* 87 (5): 366–379.

——. (2003). Mental health of refugee children: comparative study, *British Medical Journal,* 327: 134.

Gallagher, E. B., Wadsworth, A. L. and Stratton, T. D. (2002). Religion, spirituality, and mental health, *The Journal of Nervous and Mental Disease,* 190 (10): 697–704.

Gerrish, K. (2001). The nature and effect of communication difficulties arising from interactions between district nurses and South Asian patients and their carers, *Journal of Advanced Nursing,* 33: 566–574.

Goffman, E. (1963). *Stigma: Notes on the Management of Spoiled Identity.* London: Penguin Books.

Hargreaves, S., Holmes, A. and Friedland, J. (2003). The United Kingdom's experience of providing health care for refugees: time for international standards? *Journal of Travel Medicine,* 10 (2): 72–74.

Hodes, M. (2000). Psychologically distressed refugee children in the United Kingdom. *Child Psychology & Psychiatry Review,* 5 (2): 57–68.

Jones, L. and Kafetsios, K. (2002). Assessing adolescent mental health in war-affected societies: the significance of symptoms, *Child Abuse & Neglect,* 26 (10): 1059–1080.

Kaufert J. M. (1990) Sociological and anthropological perspectives on the impact of interpreters on clinician/client communication. *Santé Culture Health,* VII (2–3): 209–235.

Lamb, C. F. and Smith, M. (2002). Problems that refugees face when accessing health services, *New South Wales Public Bulletin,* 13 (7): 161–163.

Lavender, T. (2003). Redressing the balance: the place, history and future of reflective practice in clinical training, *Clinical Psychology,* 27: 11–15.

Loughry, M. and Flouri, E. (2001). The behavioural and emotional problems of former unaccompanied refugee children 3–4 years after their return to Vietnam, *Child Abuse & Neglect,* 25: 249–263.

Mckelvey, R. S. and Webb, J. A. (1995). Unaccompanied status as a risk factor in Vietnamese Amerasians, *Social Science and Medicine,* 41 (2): 261–266.

Mekki-Berrada, A., Rosseau, C. and Bertot, J. (2001). Research on refugees: means of transmitting suffering and forging social bonds,*International Journal of Mental Health*, 30 (2): 41–57.

Myers, A. (2001). Growing up too fast 16 and 17 year olds; the Leaving Care Act, *Exile*, October, 2001: 20.

Papadopoulos, R. (2001). Refugee families: issues of systemic supervision, *Journal of Family Therapy*, 23 (4): 405–422.

——. (2002). (ed.) *Therapeutic Care for Refugees: No Place Like Home*. London: Karnac.

——. (2003). Narratives of translating-interpreting with refugees: the subjugation of individual discourses. In R. Tribe and H. Raval (eds), *Working with Interpreters in Mental Health*. London: Brunner-Routledge.

Patel, N. (2003). Speaking with the silent: addressing issues of disempowerment when working with refugee people. In R. Tribe and H. Raval (eds), *Working with Interpreters in Mental Health*. London: Brunner-Routledge.

Patel, N., Bennett, E., Dennis, M., Dosanjh, N., Mahtani, A., Miller, A. and Nairdshaw, Z. (2000) *Clinical Psychology 'Race' and Culture: A Training Manual*. Leicester: British Psychological Society Books.

Podgore, J. K., René, A., Sandhu, R. and Marshall, M. (2003). A health assessment of refugee children from former Yugoslavia in Terrant Country, *Texas Medicine*, 99 (6): 50–53.

Qouta, S., Punamaki, R. and Sarraj, E. (2005). Mother-child expression of psychological distress in acute war trauma. *Clinical Child Psychology and Psychiatry*, 10 (2): 135–156.

Raval, H. (1996). A systemic perspective on working with interpreters, *Clinical Child Psychology and Psychiatry*, 1: 29–43.

——. (2002). Interpreters as co-workers: why is this relationship hard to achieve? *Context*, 59: 13–15.

——. (2003). An overview of the issues in the work with interpreters. In R. Tribe and H. Raval (eds), *Working with Interpreters in Mental Health*. London: Brunner-Routledge.

——. (2005). Being heard in the context of seeking asylum and refuge: communication with the help of bilingual co-workers,*Clinical Child Psychology and* Psychiatry, 10 (2): 197–216.

Raval, H. and Smith, J. A. (2003). Therapists' experiences of working with language interpreters, *International Journal of Mental Health*, 32: 6–32.

Raval, H. and Maltby, M. (2005). Not lost in translation: establishing a working alliance with bilingual workers and interpreters. In C. Flaskas, B. Mason and A. Perlesz (eds), *The Space between: Experience, Context and Process in the Therapeutic Relationship*. London: Karnac.

Riddell-Heaney, J. and Allott, M. (2003). Safeguarding children: 4. Needs of refugees and asylum seekers, *Professional Nurse*, 18 (9): 533–536.

Rousseau, C. (1995). The mental health of refugee children, *Transcultural Psychiatric Review*, 32: 299–331.

Rousseau, C., Said, T., Gangé, M-J. and Bibeau, G. (1998). Resilience in unaccompanied minors from the north of Somalia, *Psycholoanalytic Review*, 85 (4): 615–637.

Shelton, D. (2003). The president's new freedom commission on mental health: significance for children, *Journal of Paediatric Nursing*, 18 (3): 203–205.

Slodnjak, V., Kos, A. and Yule, W. (2002). Depression and para-suicide in refugee and Slovenian adolescents, *Crisis* 23 (3), 127–132.

Smail, D. (1990). Design for a post-behaviourist clinical psychology, *Clinical Psychology Forum*, 22: 2–10.

Sourander, A. (1998). Behaviour problems and traumatic events of unaccompanied refugee minors, *Child Abuse & Neglect*, 22 (7): 719–727.

Tribe, R. and Raval, H. (2003). (eds), *Working with InterpretersiIn Mental Health*. London: Brunner-Routledge.

Tufnell, G. (2003). Refugee children, trauma and the law, *Clinical Child Psychology and Psychiatry*, 8 (4): 431–443.

Turner, S. W., Bowie, C., Dunn, G., Shapo, L. and Yule, W. (2003). Mental health of Kosovan Albanian refugees, *British Journal of Psychiatry*, 182: 444–448.

Wahlsten, V. S., Ahmad, A. and Von Knorring, A-L. (2002). Do Kurdistanian and Swedish parents differ in their rating of competence and behavioural problems? *Nordic Journal of Psychiatry*, 56 (4): 279–283.

Weine, S. M., Raina, D., Zubi, M., Delesi, M., Huseni, D., Feetham, S., Kulauzovic, Y., Mermelstein, R., Campbell, R., Rolland, J. and Pavkovic, I. (2003). The TAFES multi-family group intervention for Kosovar refugees: a feasibility study, *The Journal of Nervous and Mental Disease*, 191 (2): 100–107.

Whittaker, S., Hardy, G., Lewis, K. and Buchan, L. (2005). An exploration of psychological well-being with young Somali refugee and asylum seeking women'. *Clinical Child Psychology and Psychiatry*, 10 (2): 177–196.

CHAPTER 6

Groupwork with Unaccompanied Young Women

Grace Heaphy, Kimberly Ehntholt and Irene Sclare

Introduction

This chapter reviews key messages from research related to the mental and emotional health of young unaccompanied refugees. Recent psychological research indicates that unaccompanied minors are at great risk of developing emotional and mental health problems as a result of traumatic experiences in their country of origin and the challenges of being alone in the United Kingdom. Despite these experiences however, the majority of young refugees are surprisingly resilient. The chapter outlines research findings which indicate that social support is an important factor in promoting resilience and in protecting against the development of psychopathology following traumatic and stressful events.

How these findings influenced the work of a specialist mental health project for young refugees is discussed. The project is described and the rationale for creating group interventions within a psychosocial framework set out. The content of a series of clinic-based group sessions is outlined, along with a description of the parallel community support offered by a social development worker. The groups aimed to help by encouraging effective coping mechanisms and building resilience, through shared problem solving and creating a friendship network. The extent to which the groups met these aims is reflected upon by drawing on feedback from the young people themselves and from the observations of the project team.

The research context

Much of the available research suggests that young refugees are a particularly vulnerable group and at great risk of experiencing psychological difficulties.

For example, Hodes (2000) has estimated that up to 40 per cent of young refugees living in the United Kingdom are experiencing mental health difficulties such as post traumatic stress disorder (PTSD), depression and anxiety. Grief reactions, as well as difficulty in sleeping and concentrating are also noted as occurring in greater frequency than within indigenous populations (Yule, 1998). Moreover, unaccompanied minors have been found to display more symptoms of psychological distress than children and young people who have sought asylum with their families (Felsman et al., 1990; Fox et al., 1994). This may be due to multiple losses and traumatic experiences as well as the stressful life circumstances unaccompanied minors often face on their own in the host country. Research confirms that one of the main difficulties for unaccompanied children is the process of asylum seeking itself, which appears to result in elevated stress levels and greater psychological difficulties (McKelvey and Webb, 1997; Silove et al., 1997; Sourander, 1998).

However, when considering research on young refugees and mental health, it must also be acknowledged that compared to studies of coping and resilience among child refugees, documentation of psychopathology is more abundant (Lustig et al., 2004). Summerfield (1999) argues that assessments of war-affected youths typically measure loss and adversity and that this perspective can downplay and distort child refugees' resilience and strengths. Despite past losses and traumatic events, difficult experiences while fleeing the country of origin, as well as ongoing stressful life experiences in the United Kingdom, the majority of young refugees are surprisingly resilient (Rutter, 2003). Social support is widely viewed as an important factor, which protects against the development of psychopathology following any traumatic or stressful event. It therefore seems possible that those refugee children who are experiencing psychological difficulties may also be the ones whose levels of social support are relatively impoverished. This would be consistent with findings from studies conducted with refugees which show that low levels of social support are associated with psychiatric disorders (Hauff and Vaglum, 1995). In one study, a reduction in social networks predicted adolescent depression better than exposure to war-related events (Farhood et al., 1993). The psychological literature contains consistent evidence that the presence of a close friend and confidant has a major buffering effect against stress (Cohen and Mills, 1985). Fox and colleagues (1994) have shown that the availability of support systems facilitated the successful adaptation of refugee children even if they had experienced extreme violence and trauma. Another study also found a positive relationship between social support and adjustment in adolescent refugees (Kovacev and Shute, 2004). Adolescents who reported having close friends to rely on had higher global self-worth and viewed themselves as more socially acceptable.

Unaccompanied minors are forced to flee their country of origin for a number of reasons related to war (Ayotte and Williamson, 2001). As part of the process of departure they are cut off from all previous sources of social support including family, friends and other community groups such as educational or religious organisations (Sourander, 1998). With greater acknowledgement of the importance of social relationships and the impact of the social world on an individual, more interest in the development of psychosocial programmes for refugee children has been generated, aimed at rebalancing and regenerating safe and sustaining connections between people and their social environments, and moving away from more individualised models of responding to psychological distress (Loughry and Eyber, 2004). Seltzer (2004) offers a critique of individual-based mental health interventions and instead suggests that greater emphasis should be placed on more broadly based psychosocial interventions because individualised models of assistance may not do justice to the complexity of the needs being presented.

Mindful of the research quoted above, developing psychosocial group interventions seemed an appropriate response to the needs of the young refugees we worked with at the Young Refugee Mental Health Project, which we introduce below.

The young refugee mental health project

We are mental health professionals with training in different theoretical models, who worked together on the Young Refugee Mental Health Project for three years. The project was funded by the Department of Health and based within the Child and Adolescent Mental Health Services (CAMHS) of the South London & Maudsley NHS Trust. In broad terms the aims of the project were to develop innovative approaches to supporting the mental well-being of young refugees and to improve access to mental health services.

Approximately half of referrals to the project were unaccompanied young people referred for individual help. In addition to the individual treatment approaches we offered, psychosocial group interventions seemed a relevant additional response to their needs. We hoped to develop an approach which combined a dual focus on increasing social support and alleviating emotional distress through the sharing of thoughts, worries and coping strategies. We shared Woodcock's view (1997) that groupwork offers opportunities for the processes of resilience to be brought forth in an accessible way and enhanced. The group, as he suggests, offers a micro-climate of support, within which practical and emotional strategies for survival and resettlement can be exchanged between members and between members and facilitators.

Working cross-culturally

As a team of white non-refugee professionals, we wanted from the outset to pay close attention to the challenges and possibilities inherent in cross-cultural work (Mason and Sawyerr, 2002). For example, we were aware that the cross-cultural validity of diagnostic categories has been brought into question and in relation to refugee mental health the debate has crystallised around trauma and the diagnosis of PTSD (Bracken and Petty, 1998). Current discourses around trauma incorporate assumptions about suffering and healing which may not be universally valid, and as Bracken (1998) points out, Western psychiatry is a particular, culturally based, way of thinking about and responding to mental distress. Discussing the connection between psychosocial impairment and symptoms Barenbaum and colleagues (2004) observe that an increasing amount of research has found that whether or not psychological symptoms will be perceived as distressing is greatly influenced by the individual interpretations of the traumatic experience and the context in which it occurs.

Therefore rather than assuming linear causations between extreme events (Woodcock, 2000) and outcomes that create a diagnostically based understanding of the young people from a Western paradigm, our preference was to learn to pay attention to the meaning young people gave to their own experiences. For us, not assuming that we knew, but remaining open to the many possible explanations and understandings of people's experiences, allowed for more 'culture-specific ways of understanding, expressing and healing' (Dawes, 2000 quoted in Barenbaum et al., 2004: 46).

Dyche and Zayas (1995) suggest that adopting a position of respectful curiosity and maintaining a disciplined attitude of cultural naïveté is helpful, as is a stance of 'not knowing', described by Anderson and Goolishian (1992: 29) as 'a general attitude ... in which the therapist's actions communicate an abundant, genuine curiosity ... a need to know more ... rather than convey preconceived opinions and expectations about the client, the problem or what must be changed'. The worker is always in a state of being informed by the client; is always *in the process* of understanding (Cecchin, 1987).

Whilst these ideas informed our work, other practices also assisted our endeavours to work in culturally sensitive ways. Having some knowledge of the country of origin and cultural practices of group members appeared to be informative. This information however needed to be held lightly; held as a possibility rather than truth, so as to avoid the problems of stereotyping. Requesting assistance and advice from members of communities with whom we were working, akin to Waldegrave and Tamaseses' (1994) notion of 'cultural consultants' appeared to us to be a useful practice. For example, when working with the Ugandan group, the facilitators conferred regularly with a colleague from that country, who advised on specific cultural practices and offered another perspective on issues that arose in the group. However, we were also mindful of not wanting to over-value cultural relativism, when some important universal experiences for refugee children also needed to be borne in mind. Barenbaum et al.'s (2004) suggestion that relativism and universalism have a co-dependant and dynamic relationship struck us as an important idea in the context of working with refugee children. For example, the range of symptoms presented by young people referred to our project were strikingly similar despite them coming from divergent cultural backgrounds. Finally, we were encouraged by Burnham and Harris's (1996) advice to make a start and be prepared to learn from our clients and our mistakes rather than feel that we had to become experts on all cultures.

Planning the groups

Interviews with unaccompanied minors living in London revealed that they wanted contact with adults who could understand their particular experiences and could offer safety and support; opportunities to engage with important aspects of their culture, such as eating 'home food' and connections to networks of social support. Education was seen as a key factor in their lives and social activities were important as a way of managing anxieties and gaining support in relation to the complex problems they faced (Williamson, 1998). This resonated clearly with what we heard directly from unaccompanied minors in our clinical work and influenced our thinking in setting up the groups. As a result, the groups included opportunities to eat and socialise together, the availability of a support worker throughout and also after the group, and the group sessions were aimed at helping young people make sense of their complex experiences. Other considerations also shaped our planning.

The local need

A number of unaccompanied, mostly newly arrived young women, some of whom had babies or were pregnant, were identified by local professional networks (Social Services Asylum teams, Connexions, Refugee Council, Child and Adolescent Mental Health Services, GPs and paediatricians) as having high social and psychological needs. Although some social groups had been initiated locally for young men who were refugees, the lack of any additional support for young women, alongside our knowledge of high levels of sexual assault experienced by the young women led to decisions to run single sex groups, first for Eritrean and Ethiopian young women and later for young women from Uganda. Having a high number of referrals from the same country (Uganda) enabled us to form a single country group; the young women from Eritrea/ Ethiopia were all of dual heritage and were referred in sufficient numbers to form a group.

Working in partnership with other service providers

The project had close ties with a similarly funded refugee project whose remit was to assist young refugees in accessing social, educational and health resources. This, coupled with an awareness of the extensive practical problems that unaccompanied minors frequently encounter related to housing, legal issues, access to financial support, education and career advice (Stanley, 2001), led us to invite a colleague from that team – a social development worker – to join in our group work initiative. There were many strands to her role in the group. These included advocacy and helping to access appropriate health, education, legal, financial and leisure resources. This was especially important for those more newly arrived. This role supplemented and added to that of the young people's social workers, who were variable in the extent of support they were offering. The social development worker was available between group sessions to visit young people and accompany them to appointments; she encouraged group attendance by reminding group members of the day and time of the meetings; she provided support between sessions where there were worries about risk and offered advice when young people reached 18 years and were faced with a number of other transitions – financial, educational, legal.

Creating the groupwork team

In addition to group facilitators, the project team had inputs from an inter-preter, supervisor and group consultant. Groups were run with two facilitators: one mental health professional and the social development worker. There were many benefits to this arrangement. For example, facilitators were embedded in different networks of professional relationships which allowed for recruiting to the group from a wide range of sources. This fitted well with the project's brief to create and improve access to mental health services for young refugees.

Gaining an initial understanding of the young women's lives

As a first contact, the social development worker met with each young person in either their own home or in a community setting. In addition to getting to know the young women and discussing the group, she assessed degrees of social capital. By this we mean 'those factors promoting social coherence and integration inherent in social systems, such as kinship and the family ... friendship and mutual support in local social, political and religious groups' (Garland et al., 2002: 71).

These individual interviews in familiar settings, helped to facilitate engage-ment and to assist us in gaining an initial understanding of the young women's current life circumstances. We discovered that although they were on the whole socially isolated, with little or no peer or adult support, the majority regularly attended college and religious institutions.

The context in which groups are run will inevitably shape their form. Working within a mental health context where our responsibilities include assessing risk and vulnerability led us to also conduct a thorough assessment of each individual's functioning from a mental health perspective, prior to the beginning of the group. Each young person met with a team member from the Young Refugee Mental Health Project in order to discuss the nature of the group in more detail, their current social and psychological needs, as well as their strengths and hopes for the future.

Drawing from clinical experience, we were attuned to the potential mental and emotional stresses experienced by young women seeking asylum. We enquired about areas of concern and distress for the young women and each young woman was asked to complete psychological self-report questionnaires. These questionnaires were intended to measure any change as a result of the group intervention. They were also used to alert us to those group members who might be in need of additional and perhaps more intensive input and support.

The interviews and questionnaires indicated that the young women were experiencing depressed mood, high levels of anxiety and symptoms of PTSD such as nightmares, sleep difficulties and frequent upsetting, intrusive thoughts about past events. Despite often very high levels of emotional distress, few had been referred for any additional support by either their social worker or GP. This oversight could be partially explained by high levels of functioning in other areas such as education.

Conducting detailed first interviews made it possible for group facilitators to remain sensitised to each young person's circumstances and to notice and respond to any deterioration in mood or a decreased ability to cope. Speaking to each young person also helped the facilitators identify shared experiences and themes in the young people's lives, which could be held in mind when considering possible topics or activities for the group sessions.

During these individual interviews the young women shared often painful and traumatic past experiences. All had been separated from families or their families had been killed as a result of political instability in their countries of origin. Many had witnessed the killing of immediate family members, including parents and siblings. The majority of the young women from Uganda had been raped; some had been held in rebel camps where they were forced to work and repeatedly physically and sexually assaulted; others were pregnant or had a child as a result of rape; one young woman was trafficked to the United Kingdom where she was held in captivity and forced to work as a prostitute. These descriptions concur with Thomas et al.'s (2004) findings in a study of pre-flight experiences of unaccompanied asylum seeking children: their most prominent finding being that some form of violence was the primary reason for flight in almost all cases; a third of young people reported being raped before leaving their country of origin, with this rising to 24 per cent for African girls and 13 per cent had witnessed the death or execution of family members.

In these individual meetings most of the young women seemed willing and at times eager to talk about events and experiences leading up to their arrival in the United Kingdom, but were reluctant to do so in the group setting. There may be many reasons for this, one being the nature of the young women's experiences which for many involved rape. Feelings of shame and stigma were possible factors in preventing these otherwise open and animated young women from sharing with peers (Medical Foundation Child and Adolescent Psychotherapy Team, 2004). Kohli's view (2006) that maintaining silence may be a protective strategy and a way of concealing and managing hurt is also relevant here. This avoidance of discussions about the past was, however, in contrast to our experiences conducting other types of school-based groups for young refugees (Ehntholt et al., 2005), during which the participants were usually eager to talk about and share very distressing past experiences, such as witnessing amputations in Sierra Leone or the shooting of neighbours in Kosovo.

In summary we conducted these holistic assessments with the young women with the aim of emphasising their strengths and their resilience but not negating their vulnerabilities (Rousseau et al., 2005). In these initial interviews we sought out strengths and abilities and found that despite experiencing high levels of psychological distress, these young women were managing well in their daily lives and held high hopes for their futures. Understanding that these young women were strong, resilient *and also* vulnerable shaped how we thought about the groups. Anderson (2004: 58) suggests, 'being able to identify conditions and factors which support resilience would be a central component of any type of intervention aimed at helping refugees', and this was a core idea influencing the aims and structure of the groups, given our own ethical positions and theoretical and clinical influences.

Collaborative approach

An overall approach that valued the 'expertise' of both group members and facilitators was favoured. This is usefully referred to as a collaborative approach (Anderson and Goolishian, 1992), where value is given to the knowledge of all involved in the group process. The idea of facilitators and group participants together constructing the sessions militates against a colonising effect of overvaluing group facilitators' knowledge and gives equal value to that of participants. In this context, facilitators' expertise could be described as 'creating a space and a process' in which the facilitators' professional knowledge is combined with the young women's expertise on their own lives: what they needed, hoped and wished for from the group.

With this in mind sessions were planned one week ahead with the intention of using feedback from the group to determine the content of the following session, and to stay attuned to the preferred ways of working that were evolving. Part of this collaborative style involved encouraging participants to think together about possible ways the group could be useful for them, *as well as* including ideas from group facilitators. In a group where participants do not know each other, are newly arrived in the country, may be unfamiliar with the notion of groupwork and whose cultural styles of interacting with adults may lead to a reticence to put their ideas forward, this is not a straightforward task. What proved useful in the Ugandan group was the explicit exploration of the possible meanings being in a group had for the young women, and how past experiences of membership of a group might influence participation in this group. In the first session facilitators enquired into this by raising the following questions:

- When was the last time you were in a group with others your own age?
- What was the purpose?
- How was the group run?
- What were the rules in the group?
- Who made them?
- What was the relationship between adults and young people?
- Who mostly decided what went on?

This allowed for an exploration of participants' experiences of being in group settings, the rules that applied and the relationship between adults and young people. It allowed also for the introduction of ideas from group facilitators about other possible ways of being in a group. Working cross-culturally, where shared meanings cannot be taken as given, this seems to be a particularly important conversation to engage in at the outset. This discussion allowed for an explicit negotiation of areas where this group might connect with participants' past experiences and where it might differ.

It emerged in later sessions that many of the participants had been fearful and anxious about attending this group. They had little idea of what to expect despite previous discussions with referrers, but came in response to a request from their social workers whom they trusted. This negotiating in the first session set the tone for further sessions, where mutual negotiation became a feature of the group and was encouraged throughout the life of the group.

Group structure

Groups were held for 12 sessions. Nine young women were accepted for each group with an average attendance of six at each session. Many practical issues such as transport, meetings with solicitors and social workers, and college commitments contributed to non-attendance. Almost invariably however, apologies were sent to the group, facilitated by the social development worker's contact with members outside of group sessions. Sessions were planned for 1.5 hours, although this was often extended due to lateness, and group members' reluctance to finish. Facilitators agreed that some flexibility was useful, and it seemed important to respond to the young women's needs. The high priority given to education by most unaccompanied minors influenced the decision to hold groups after 5pm.

The group format remained the same each week, beginning with a name game and variations on this; an 'icebreaker'; an introduction to the main theme of the session; an activity to explore the theme and a closing circle where participants were encouraged to say something appreciative about one another.

These group rituals proved important in providing a sense of safety, security and predictability for the exploration of various aspects of group members' experiences, but the structure was not so rigid as to be constraining. On one occasion for example, events in Uganda were high on news and press agendas. This sparked spontaneous discussions in the group related to politics and war. This continued for a large part of the session with the original plan postponed. More than once when it seemed an aspect of the session (icebreaker/closing circle) might be forgotten or passed over, a young person was quick to remind the group of its omission. One important group ritual was eating together and snacks, drinks and hot food were shared before the session began.

Creating the agenda

An aim of the groups was to decrease isolation through developing social contacts but also importantly, through allowing for a sharing of young people's experiences. Creating a context where trust could be developed was vital to this process, as was participants' sense of choice in what they disclosed. An early session was devoted to encouraging young women to 'set the agenda' for further meetings. The process of this seemed crucial, as group members were being encouraged to take some risks in sharing their worries and concerns, possibly disclosing painful aspects of their lives. Participants were asked to do the following:

- In pairs, share current worries and concerns that you would like to address in the group.
- Write these anonymously on cards, and place around the room.
- Walk around the room, viewing the array of 'worries' and 'concerns' and place a mark on the card if the concern also applies to you.

Group members then returned to the large group. Together the group graded the cards in relation to their importance – those cards with many marks were presumably concerns shared by many of the group members. A discussion ensued about which concern's participants wished to pursue in future sessions. For example, a number of participants had marked being unable to relax and feeling stressed. It was agreed we would focus on relaxation in the next session.

This exercise had a number of effects: group members themselves identified what they would like help with; they were free to set out their concerns at whatever level they chose, sharing as much or a little about themselves as they wished; young people had an opportunity to let others know about difficult aspects of their lives, without necessarily talking about them; the group developed a sense of shared and common concerns and the young women were beginning to develop an awareness of the commonality of some of their current and past experiences. They identified the follwing as current worries: 'how to relax especially when feeling stressed; my future; having bad dreams and nightmares; personal problems hard to discuss; loneliness; being alone in the nation (being unaccompanied); sleepless nights; lack of concentration; how to budget the money I am given; the direction the world is taking – politics.'

This session proved to be an important marker in the group's development, as the young women understood that concerns which had been identified by individuals were common to almost all group members.

Themes and processes

Relaxation/coping with stress

One theme identified through the above exercise was that of difficulties in relaxing, feeling stressed and problems with sleep. The following exercise was used with the intention of further exploring these difficulties and bringing forth and sharing resources in the group for managing and coping. A 'body map' was created by drawing the outline of a young person's body as she lay on a large sheet of paper. Group members were asked to

- Think about where you feel tension and stress in your body.
- Indicate this by drawing/writing on the relevant part of the body map, choose colours that best represent the experience.

Group members were then asked to share what worked for them in relieving stress. They shared practices such as reading passages of religious texts; using certain herbs and oils; engaging in physical activities and sport. Group facilitators demonstrated progressive muscle relaxation as another possibility. Participants agreed to try one of the above suggestions in the coming week. The following week, one participant reported she had done more physical activities, some had repeated the progressive muscle relaxation and another had talked more to friends. All of these were experienced as helpful in feeling less stressed.

This session led to a mutual recognition that all group members experienced some physical, emotional and psychological discomfort, such as body pain, depression (one group member's description of the black squiggles she had drawn on the head of the 'body'), and grief. This proved to be a powerful experience for many group members, evidenced by a silent attention and concentration as each member added her writing/drawing to the map. This was for some the first time they had shared this information with peers. Their experiences were reframed as normal and 'to be expected' given the difficulties of participants' lives.

In a later session group members were encouraged to create a 'safe place'. They were led through a visualisation exercise, imagining a place where they felt calm, secure and safe. They were asked to draw or paint this scene and to practice using their imagination to return to this safe place when they felt unsettled or needed to relax. Some members reported using this technique to assist a return to sleep after upsetting dreams.

Identifying strengths

In an earlier session another theme explored was that of participants' strengths. Group members were asked to share in pairs 'what kept them strong' and what strengths they themselves had. In a large group, members made collages to represent these strengths. These included representations of God, of family, and of learning and education. When completed, these were taped together to make one large group banner, which was displayed at each meeting. This was a symbolic and visual representation of group members' resilience and ability to survive and endure, and was referred to often during subsequent sessions.

Adjusting to life in the United Kingdom

Group members were encouraged to share their stories of adjusting to a new country. Some young women expressed an interest in meeting with a person from their country of origin who was now successfully settled in the United Kingdom. In a later session, a young professional, herself a refugee, was invited to attend the group and share her experiences. This was highly valued by group members who said that this had been their favourite session. Practical aspects of adjusting to life in London were also addressed in an earlier session that focused on developing practical skills for travelling around the city. Group members played a board game called the 'Underground Game', which facilitated a more solid connection with the city's landscape. Group members and facilitators shared information about specialist food shops or places of interest or importance to the young people and these were marked on a large map. This was added to over the following weeks as group members further explored the city.

A time line of life events /a 'life map'

In another session, a 'time line' was used to map young peoples' journeys from their country of origin to the United Kingdom. The exercise was done in pairs, with group members then sharing as much or as little as they wished with the larger group. This session occurred later in the life of the group when group members already had built a sense of trust together. Participants appeared to appreciate and enjoy this opportunity to share their personal stories – creating narratives that actively sought to connect the past, present and future. In addition, much enthusiastic conversation was had about similarities of positive experiences (school, sport), and a respectful quiet understanding shown when members referred to 'difficult times' or included dates when they had lost parents and siblings.

Processes of sharing

Throughout, participants shared as much as was comfortable for them about their lives. Distressing events shared previously with facilitators were understandably not articulated but often alluded to. As Papadopoulos states: 'respecting that certain experiences had to be shared in silence (due to their unspeakable horror and inhumanity) there were times when in an unspoken way we were honouring the unutterable' (1999: 112). Instead group members found other ways to explore and refer to past events and current preoccupations. In one group where the majority of participants had experiences of rape and sexual assault, a young woman spoke about recent news from her country about the rape of a boy. A detailed discussion ensued, with some members voicing feelings of outrage and despair about the event. Some of the group were vocal and others utterly silent but paying close attention to what was being said. Keeping the focus strictly to this event involving someone of the opposite gender seemed to provide a safe enough distance from their own experiences to allow an acknowledgement of what had also happened to them. The group had somehow found a manageable way to name and explore a significant experience common to many, without compromising each other's privacy.

Endings

For young people who have often endured multiple losses and unplanned disruptions to their lives, allowing time to prepare and plan for the group ending seemed crucial. Group members themselves decided how they would like to come together for a final occasion. They suggested preparing and eating food from their home country and playing and dancing to music from the United Kingdom and their countries of origin. Facilitators organised an exercise resulting in each young person taking home a small jar filled with messages of appreciation from other group members. Photographs were taken and later shared by the young people themselves. Importantly some time was spent exchanging telephone numbers and planning for future social contact.

Evaluation and reflections

A number of methods were used to evaluate the groups, including individual interviews with the young women, a focus group conducted by an independent facilitator and a group evaluation discussion led by group facilitators. We set out some of the young women's comments and feedback below, but first reflect on some of our experiences as group facilitators.

Co-working and facilitators' relationships

There were many positive aspects of developing the group with facilitators from different professional backgrounds. The role taken up by the social development worker was crucial in maintaining a more seamless experience for the young women, whose needs were wide ranging and crossed physical, psychological and social boundaries. The social development worker was available between sessions to support group members in various ways and her accessibility was greatly enhanced through the use of text messaging, which worked extremely well and was widely used by group members.

A sense of continuity between group sessions was created for the young women, which generated feelings of being cared for and being held in mind outside of the group time. As one young woman stated in an evaluation interview: 'it mattered whether we came to this group – in other groups nobody cared whether we came or not'.

At times, facilitators held different views on aspects of the group's running which was perhaps attributable to differences in professional backgrounds and models of working. For example, the social development worker expressed some reservations about whether a full assessment of mental health needs was necessary before the group began.

In one sense one facilitator held the mental/emotional health aspect of the young women's experiences, while the other held the social aspects. On the whole this worked. However, our experience highlights the need to ensure there is enough agreement between facilitators on the overall aims of the group and how these should be achieved, so that the tasks are understood and shared jointly as much as possible (Reynolds and Shackman, 1994). Inevitably there were areas of divergence, and it is here that regular supervision was essential.

Supervision has a number of purposes and provides opportunities to review and plan sessions, share responses to what facilitators have encountered in sessions on a practical and emotional level and consider the working relationship of facilitators. Woodcock (2001) suggests that when working with refugees time should be taken to consider the issues and emotions that arise for workers. He suggests that the enormity of the challenges faced by refugees can contribute to a huge sense of dependence and reliance on the worker: it is important therefore that workers have good support so they can be enabled to continue offering psychological and also practical help. Fostering the resilience of workers is also an important element of supervision: having safe spaces and secure relationships (both peer and supervisory) can enhance workers' creativity and also allow for respectful challenging of the work where necessary (Avigad, 2003).

The young women's reflections

Many of the young women indicated that the groups had been helpful to them on a number of levels. They made comments such as 'it felt like home', said they appreciated being in the company of others from the same country, sharing food and having opportunities to 'speak our language'. A majority of the young women felt they had more confidence following attendance at the group. One young woman who had been extremely isolated, fearful and mistrustful, commented that the group now made it possible for her to talk to others and to consider joining another group (a drop-in). Prior to her experiences in this group she explained she was 'too terrified' and 'didn't know how to talk' with others. This suggests an increase in group members' emotional capital, that is, 'those internal resources that determine an individual's capacity to relate to and connect with other human beings' (Garland et al., 2002: 90). Indeed the development of emotional capital can add to the social capital of young people by increasing their capacity to make use of whatever is available to them through social networks.

Some strong relationships were created in the groups, which continued many months after the groups ended. These included one-to-one friendships and small groups who socialised together. For some these were the first friendships formed since arrival in the country. The strength of these ties is illustrated by the following: shortly after one group ended one young woman gave birth and invited another to become godmother to her child. This was the only friend she had in this country and this new relationship further strengthened their bond. A year later, the godmother plays a very active part in the child's life.

The young women also valued 'gaining knowledge' in the groups: they valued 'being taught new things' and liked learning from facilitators and from one another.

The young women did not share our concern that facilitators were not of the same cultural backgrounds as group members. One young person clearly stated that for her, having facilitators from the host country organising the group conveyed an interest and a welcoming attitude, which she would not necessarily have felt had the group been run by people from her country.

Regarding gender- and culture-specific groups, the overwhelming view was that young women were open to the idea of mixed culture groups but unanimously favoured being in an all-female group. Finally, without exception, group members were of the opinion that the groups were too short – a view we shared as facilitators. The project's time and resource limitations did not allow for longer commitment but undoubtedly this is an area that would require serious reconsideration in planning future groups.

Overall, the psychosocial frame of the groups facilitated connection with diverse aspects of young peoples' lives, which went some way towards meeting our aim of providing therapeutic services that 'weave into [young people's] ordinary experiences, rather than being offered as part of a refined and intensive "therapeutic encounter" ' (Kohli and Mather, 2003: 206). There was some realisation of our hopes that the groups could provide a space where young unaccompanied refugees could begin to re-gather the threads of their lives and weave together something useful to them in their continuing journey.

References

Anderson, A. (2004). Resilience. In R. Hamilton and D. Moore (eds), *Educational Interventions for Refugee Children*. London: Routledge Falmer.

Anderson, H. and Goolishian, H. (1992). The client is the expert: a not-knowing approach to therapy. In S. McNamee and K. Gergen (eds), *Therapy as Social Construction*. London: Sage.

Avigad, J. (2003). On becoming a supervisor to teams working with survivors of torture, *Context*, 67: 26–28.

Ayotte, W. and Williamson, L. (2001). *Separated Children in the UK. An Overview of the Current Situation*. London: Save the Children.

Barenbaum, J., Ruchkin, V. and Schwab-Stone, M. (2004). The psychosocial aspects of children exposed to war: practice and policy initiatives, *Journal of Child Psychology and Psychiatry*, 10 (1): 41–62.

Bracken, P. (1998). Hidden agendas: deconstructing post traumatic stress disorder. In P. Bracken and C. Petty (eds), *Rethinking the Trauma of War*. London: Free Association Books.

Bracken, P. and Petty, C. (eds). (1998). *Rethinking the Trauma of War*. London: Free Association Books.

Burnham, J. and Harris, Q. (1996). Emerging ethnicity. a tale of three cultures. In K. N. Dwivedi and V. Varma (eds), *Meeting the Needs of Ethnic Minority Children*. London: Jessica Kingsley.

Cecchin, G. (1987). Hypothesizing, circularity and neutrality revisited: an invitation to curiosity, *Family Process*, 20 (4): 405–413.

Cohen, S. and Mills, T. A. (1985). Stress, social support, and the buffering hypothesis. *Psychological Bulletin*, 98: 310–357.

Dawes, A. (2000). Cultural diversity and childhood adversity: implications for community level interventions with children in difficult circumstances. Presented at Children in Adversity: Ways to Reinforce the Coping Ability and Resilience of Children in Situations of Hardship, September, 2000, Oxford University.

Dyche, L. and Zayas, L. H. (1995). The value of curiosity and naïveté for the cross-cultural psychotherapist, *Family Process*, 30: 389–401.

Ehntholt, K. A., Smith, P. A. and Yule, W. (2005). School-based cognitive-behavioural therapy group intervention for refugee children who have experienced war-related trauma, *Clinical Child Psychology and Psychiatry*, 10 (2): 235–250.

Farhood, L., Zurayk, H., Chaya, M., Saadeh, F., Meshefedjian, G. and Sidani, T. (1993). 'The impact of war on the physical and mental health of the family: The Lebanese experience', *Social Science and Medicine*, 36 (12): 1555–1567.

Felsman, J. K., Leong, F. T., Johnson, M. C. and Felsman, I. C. (1990). Estimates of psychological distress among Vietnamese refugees: adolescents, unaccompanied minors and young adults, *Social Science and* Medicine, 31 (11): 1251–1256.

Fox, P. G., Cowell, J. M. and Montgomery, A. C. (1994). The effects of violence on health and adjustment of Southeast Asian refugee children: an integrative review, *Public Health Nursing*, 11 (3): 195–201.

Garland, C., Hume, F. and Majid, S. (2002). Remaking connections: refugees and the development of 'emotional capital' in therapy groups. In R. K. Papadopoulos (ed.), *Therapeutic Care for Refugees. No Place Like Home*. London: Karnac.

Hauff, E. and Vaglum, P. (1995). Organized violence and the stress of exile, predictors of mental health in a community cohort of Vietnamese refugees three years after resettlement, *British Journal of Psychiatry*, 166: 360–367.

Hodes, M. (2000). Psychologically distressed children in the United Kingdom, *Child Psychology and Psychiatry Review*, 5: 57–68.

Kohli, R. K. S. (2006). The sound of silence: listening to what unaccompanied asylum seeking children say and do not say, *British Journal of Social Work*, 36: 707–721.

Kohli, R. K. S. and Mather, R. (2003). Promoting psychosocial well-being in unaccompanied asylum seeking young people in the United Kingdom, *Child and Family Social Work*, 8: 201–212.

Kovacev, L. and Shute, R. (2004). Acculturation and social support in relation to psychosocial adjustment of adolescent refugees resettled in Australia, *International Journal of Behavioural Development*, 28 (3): 259–267.

Loughry, M. and Eyber, C. (2004). *Psychosocial Concepts in Humanitarian Work with Children: A Review of the Concepts and Related Literature*. Washington, DC: National Academy of Sciences.

Lustig, S., Kia-Keating, M., Knight, W., Geltman, P., Ellis, H., Kinzie, J., Keane, T. and Saxe, G. (2004). Review of child and adolescent refugee mental health, *Journal of the American Academy of Child & Adolescent Psychiatry*, 43 (1): 24–36.

Mason, B. and Sawyerr, A. (eds). (2002). *Exploring the Unsaid. Creativity, Risks and Dilemmas in Working Cross-Culturally*. London: Karnac.

McKelvey, R. S. and Webb, J. A. (1997). A prospective study of psychological stress related to refugee camp experience, *Australian and New Zealand Journal of Psychiatry*, 31 (4): 549–554.

Medical Foundation Child and Adolescent Psychotherapy Team. (2004). When the future has been spoilt: the impact of politically motivated rape on children and adolescents. In M. Peel (ed.), *Rape as a Method of Torture*. London: Medical Foundation for the Care of Victims of Torture.

Papadopoulos, P. (1999). Working with Bosnian medical evacuees and their families: therapeutic dilemmas, *Clinical Child Psychology and Psychiatry*, 4 (1): 107–120.

Reynolds, J. and Shackman, J. (1994). Partnership in training and practice with refugees, *Groupwork*, 7 (1): 23–36.

Rousseau, C., Drapeau, A., Lacroix, L., Bagilishya, D. and Heusch, N. (2005). Evaluation of a classroom program of creative expression workshops for refugee and immigrant children, *Journal of Child Psychology and* Psychiatry, 46 (2): 180–185.

Rutter, J. (2003). *Supporting Refugee Children in 21st Century Britain: A Compendium of Essential Information.* Stoke on Trent: Trentham Books.

Seltzer, A. (2004). Rape and mental health: the psychiatric sequel of violation as an abuse of human rights. In M. Peel (ed.), *Rape as a Method of Torture.* London: Medical Foundation for the Care of Victims of Torture.

Silove, D., Sinnerbrink, I., Field, A., Manicavasagar, V. and Steel, Z. (1997). Anxiety, depression and PTSD in asylum seekers: associations with pre-migration trauma and post-migration stressors, *British Journal of Psychiatry*, 170 (4): 351–357.

Sourander, A. (1998). Behavior problems and traumatic events of unaccompanied refugee minors, *Child Abuse and Neglect*, 22 (7): 719–727.

Stanley, K. (2001). *Cold Comfort. Young Separated Refugees in England.* London: Save the Children.

Summerfield, D. (1999). A critique of seven assumptions behind psychological trauma programmes in war-affected areas, *Social Science & Medicine*, 48: 1449–1462.

Thomas, S., Thomas, S., Nafees, B. and Bhugra, D. (2004). 'I was running away from death' – the pre-flight experiences of unaccompanied asylum seeking children in the UK, *Child: Care, Health and Development*, 30 (2): 113–122.

Waldergrave, C. and Tamasese, K. (1994). Some central ideas in the 'Just Therapy' Approach, *Human Systems*, 5: 191–208.

Williamson, L. (1998). Unaccompanied – but not unsupported. In J. Rutter and C. Jones (eds), *Refugee Education: Mapping the Field.* Stoke on Trent: Trentham Books.

Woodcock, J. (1997). Groupwork with refugees and asylum seekers. In T. Mistry and A. Brown (eds). *Race and Groupwork.* London: Whiting and Birch.

——. (2000). Refugee children and their families: theoretical and clinical perspectives. In K. Dwivedi (ed.), *Post Traumatic Stress Disorder in Children and Adolescents.* London: Whurr.

——. (2001). A dozen differences to consider when working with refugee families, *Context*, 53: 24–25.

Yule, W. (1998). The psychological adaptation of refugee children. In J. Rutter and C. Jones (eds), *Refugee Education: Mapping the Field.* Stoke on Trent: Trentham Books.

CHAPTER 7

Friends and Family Care of Unaccompanied Children: Recognising the Possible and the Potential

Maura Kearney

Introduction

Kinship care, whether formal or informal, appears to have much to offer any child who cannot be cared for by their parents. It may have a considerable amount to offer children who are not only separated from their parents and the home that is familiar to them but from *all* that is familiar to them. It is such circumstances that unaccompanied asylum seeking children are likely to experience. This chapter aims to explore how the social work profession can work with unaccompanied children and their kinship networks to enable their friends and family to provide them with care. It is possible that such friends and family care arrangements occur informally, however, this discussion focuses upon children who have been identified as 'unaccompanied asylum seeking children' and are known to social services. As a result, they become children 'in need' and the responsibility of social services. In the main, the chapter explores the development of assessment practice within one social work team based in Kent, in the South East of England.

In our experience, such assessment practice posed a number of challenges; the chapter aims to reflect on these providing a descriptive account of how our practice evolved over time. Many of these challenges resulted from the context within which we were working. Our work with unaccompanied children was overshadowed by concerns around trafficking (Somerset, 2004) and the vulnerability of children in informal care settings (Philpot, 2001, 2003). In our view, such concerns have created an environment in which adults laying claim to unaccompanied children, recently arrived in the United Kingdom, are viewed with suspicion. The willingness of practitioners, influenced by local authority policies, to engage with these adults has been limited by fear; fear that has perhaps been further exacerbated by the tragic death of Victoria Climbie, a child migrant, while living in a private fostering arrangement (Laming, 2003). Such a culture of fear and suspicion has serious implications for social workers' capacity to work collaboratively in partnership with unaccompanied children's friends, families and social networks. This is compounded further by the inherent uncertainty that exists in working with a group of children and adults who have little or no documented past and who may be reluctant or find it difficult to share stories of their past for a range of reasons.

Yet, the value of good kinship care for the well-being of an unaccompanied child is likely to be considerable. The general literature on kinship care demonstrates the value it holds for children separated from their parents (Flynn, 2000, 2002; Doolan et al., 2004; Greeff et al., 1999; Ryburn, 1998). Kohli (2003) writes of unaccompanied children as experiencing 'a series of fractures in their past, present and future lives that need to be healed' for whom 'circumstances have conspired to peel away the layers of connection, leaving them exposed and vulnerable in their new environments' (202). An adult who is known to a child or to the immediate family in their country of origin, may offer some continuity of care and may reduce the level of vulnerability that a child may experience in the new environment (Department of Health, 1995). If the adult has also left the homeland, irrespective of whether forced to do so or not, s/he is likely to have some appreciation or understanding of the child's current feelings of loss. The commonality of their experiences may offer the child the opportunity to make sense of the fractures that they have experienced.

The legal and policy context

Practice guidance on the support of unaccompanied children (Department of Health, 1995) emphasises the potential that informal care arrangements and links to friends and relatives in the community may offer children and young people. Three key points are made in the guidance, although each is premised on the priority that must be given to their 'absolute right to be protected from neglect and/or abuse of any kind' (10). It advises that where informal care arrangements exist 'there should be a strong bias, other things being equal, towards finding *imaginative ways* to support the continuity of that placement'(16); 'if, after a considered assessment, these arrangements are not thought to be viable *every effort* should be made to explore whether there are other relatives or friends able, with support, to care properly for these children' (10), and 'even *where there is no option other than to accommodate* the child or take care proceedings every effort should be made to maintain the child's relationships with caring and interested friends and relatives in the community' (10).

In essence, the guidance reiterates some of the key duties of local authorities enshrined in the Children Act 1989. First, where a child is deemed to be 'in need' the Act provides powers to safeguard and promote the welfare of such children within their area. So far as is consistent with that duty the local authority must promote the care of children and young people by their families by providing a range and level of services appropriate to their needs (s17(1)). Second, it has a duty to provide 'accommodation' if there is no one with parental responsibility for them, or if they are lost or abandoned, or if the person who has been caring for them cannot provide suitable accommodation or care (s20(1)). A child who is being provided with 'accommodation' by a local authority (s20) (or subject to a care order (s31)) is known as a 'looked after' child. Before making any decision about a looked after child, the local authority must try to find out the wishes and feelings of the child, and those of his or her parents, anyone with parental responsibility, and anyone else whom the local authority considers relevant (s22(4)). Due consideration must be given to these opinions alongside the child's religion, racial origin, and cultural and linguistic background (s22(5)). The Act also underwrites the importance of working towards the placement of a child with an adult who is connected to them: a family member, relative, or 'other suitable person' unless 'it would not be reasonably practicable or consistent with his welfare' (s23(6)). If a child is 'looked after' the family member, relative or other suitable person should be approved as a foster carer (DOH, 2002, formerly DOH, 1991).

Unaccompanied asylum seeking children are by definition 'in need' (DOH, 1995; Kidane, 2001; DOH, 2003) and, given that there is no one with parental responsibility for them, are likely to be 'accommodated' by local authorities. Recent guidance states that

> where a child has no parent or guardian in this country, perhaps because he has arrived alone seeking asylum, the presumption should be that he would fall within the scope of section 20 and become looked after, unless the needs assessment reveals particular factors which would suggest that an alternative response would be more appropriate. While the needs assessment is being carried out, he should be cared for under section 20. (DOH, 2003: 13)

In view of this guidance and the duties and powers outlined above, there are a number of possible ways in which local authorities supporting unaccompanied children may facilitate living arrangements within their kinship networks. For example, a local authority may assess an unaccompanied child as 'in need' of being accommodated and work towards the approval of a friend or family member as a foster carer. In such circumstances, a child may live with an adult for up to six weeks, while the carers are approved (DOH, 2002). Alternatively, the needs assessment of the child and 'family' may reveal 'particular factors', which would suggest that an alternative response would be more appropriate. In these circumstances, the local authority may elect to support the arrangement, by providing a range and level of services appropriate to a child's needs, under section 17 of the Act as it may be consistent with promoting the care of children and young people by their families (s17(1)). It is also possible in some circumstances, where a child is *in situ*, that the local authority may designate it as a private fostering arrangement, as the circumstances may suggest that a child has been placed with non-related carers by their parents or relatives in an informal arrangement. Indeed, recent research has shown that local authorities have interpreted their responsibilities along these lines for different cases (Wade et al., 2005). Additionally, it is possible that these arrangements could be secured by use of Residence Orders or the Special Guardianship provisions that are due to be introduced (See Broad and Skinner, 2005 for a discussion of their terms).

One social work team's story

The team whose practice is the focus of this chapter were a small team of experienced social workers, who had been responsible for developing long-term placement resources for unaccompanied children. The team was part of Kent Asylum Service, operated by the local authority social services department. Due to the location of Dover, a major seaport, within its boundaries, it has been responsible for the arrival of large numbers of unaccompanied children. For example, in September 2001, the authority was already supporting 500 unaccompanied children and young people but this figure quadrupled within the following year (Hayes, 2002). The main relevance of this for the team's practice was the way in which these children and young people came to the attention of the department, although, of course, the volume of referrals also had some implications for practice. As the children and young people were identified at the point they entered the country, the local authority had a key role in facilitating contact with any social networks existent in the United Kingdom. In early 2001, it was clear that many children and young people were expressing a wish to get in contact, with a view to going to live, with adult friends or relatives living in the United Kingdom. However, little action was taken in these cases because the authority was at that time struggling to meet even immediate basic care needs as its first priority (Gilroy, 2001). Consequently, the placements team became responsible for the assessment of these prospective carers in a bid to give due consideration to the children and young people's wishes.

The 'test' case: Thanh Nguyen who wanted to live with his 'father'

Our first case emerged from a series of discussions between three social work team managers about a 15-year-old Vietnamese boy, who we will call the fictional name of Thanh Nguyen. He was living in a residential placement but he wished to live with an adult, Mr Nguyen, who claimed to be his father. Thanh and his 'father' had *never met* prior to the boy's arrival in the United

Kingdom. Their relationship was not documented in any way, and it was not possible to confirm their respective stories. Thanh spoke only a little English, and was isolated in his placement. He was not eating, was constantly distressed and had absconded on occasions. An alternative linguistically and culturally appropriate placement would not be easy to locate: even suggesting this to Thanh was met with a blank refusal. Thanh's social worker had already visited Mr Nguyen at home and had given permission for Thanh to stay for short visits due to his increasing vulnerability in his placement. However, the child and his 'father' wanted this to become a permanent arrangement. The use of inverted commas here is not intended to confer suspicion on Mr Nguyen but to illustrate the case as we saw it. Our team was asked to investigate and report back so that a decision could be made.

Initially, this request seemed relatively straightforward – a myriad of assessment models and procedures already existed to facilitate different kinds of placements. However, in the end, not one of them proved to be entirely appropriate. This was due mainly to the uncertainty that surrounded the identity of Mr Nguyen. It was not possible to immediately confirm that the man was Thanh's father, therefore, we felt that we were unable to definitively consider this as a placement with family. But the possibility that the man *may* be his father ruled out his assessment as a foster carer. Yet, even if it was possible to accept the man as Thanh's father, he had no 'parental responsibility' as he had never been married to Thanh's mother. It was also not possible to obtain permission from Thanh's mother, as she was believed to be dead. Mr Nguyen saw no reason to apply for a Residence Order, as he felt that as Thanh's father it was unnecessary; in any event it may not have been technically possible. Adoption was inappropriate as it was possible that Thanh's mother *may* still be alive in Vietnam or that this man *may not* be his father. It was apparent that there was no obvious legal route to pursue to formalise Thanh's placement with this man.

Yet, two things always remained clear from the outset: Thanh and Mr Nguyen wanted to be together, and Thanh was suffering in his current placement. It was with this in mind that we set out to consider how we could make the placement possible while also fulfilling our mandate of ensuring Thanh's safety and protection. It quickly became apparent that, in reality, the only material available to work with was the version of events presented by the two people concerned. We had no access to official information about the child or adult's past; there was no parent or any extended family available to expand on either story. In theory, it may have been possible to obtain information from the country of origin but this depended on the accuracy of the details provided by the informants. On this basis, it would have been difficult to assess the reliability of information provided by informal networks and it may have been difficult to identify appropriate formal agencies. Additionally, given Thanh's status as an asylum seeker, it may have been inappropriate or even dangerous to approach formal agencies in his home country.

Consequently, we planned to gather information through a series of separate interviews with the child and the adult. We had to re-consider our plan, as Thanh was too distressed to participate in any interviews. Instead, we spoke to practitioners who had come to know him, gathering information about his current situation and what he had revealed about his past. Through a series of interviews, we attempted to build a picture of: Mr Nyugen as a person, his past, his relationship to Thanh's mother, his knowledge of Thanh's childhood and his present circumstances. His account of his life in the United Kingdom over a number of years could be verified. His parenting history could be traced as well as observed, as he had other children with whom he lived. Significantly, his family members demonstrated a strong commitment to Thanh. Thanh's desire, and evident desperation, to be part of this family was a key part of the decision making throughout. He was able to express his own wishes and feelings. However, as consideration of his safety was paramount, this in itself was not regarded as a sufficient indicator of it being in his 'best interests'.

Despite the amount of information gathered, many questions remained unanswered. It was not possible to determine if Mr Nyugen was Thanh's father, or, even if he was a close relative. We considered the use of DNA but felt it inappropriate for a number of reasons. The timescales involved were too long given Thanh's level of vulnerability. However, we were also aware that DNA testing may have resolved the question as to whether or not they were biologically related but it would not have resolved the question as to whether or not they should live together (See Taitz et al., 2002 for discussion of such issues). More significantly, our assessment revealed much that was positive about this man and his family, indicating that this could potentially be a safe, appropriate and permanent placement for Thanh. The deciding factor was Thanh's determination to live with this family. The placement was recommended on the condition that social services remained involved for a specific period under section 20 of Children Act 1989, which both Thanh and his 'father' agreed to. In the following months, Thanh became visibly transformed physically and emotionally; it was abundantly clear that he was thriving in the family. The local authority therefore continued to support the arrangement under section 17 of the Children Act 1989.

Being adaptive and creative: an evolving model for assessment

This initial experience suggested that the dilemmas that we faced could not be resolved by using existing assessment frameworks. We needed to be able to address two principle objectives. First, we need to find a way of 'verifying' the nature of the relationship between the child and proposed carer. Second, although this is likely to occur simultaneously, we needed to provide a robust assessment of the proposed carer's willingness and capacity to care for and protect the child. It is the first of these objectives that is perhaps particular to working with children and adults who are asylum seeking, because there is seldom recourse to information beyond that which the participants in the assessment can provide. The following section therefore provides a descriptive overview of the assessment process as it developed.

The potential for a kinship assessment and placement begins with the identification of a child who has links to adult family members or friends living in the United Kingdom. This is dependent upon duty or allocated social workers being mindful of this possibility and/or following up on information, no matter how basic, in a bid to trace any adult or adults that the child has expressed a desire to be in contact or to live with. In our experience, it was important, for different reasons, that this was acted upon immediately. When a child is newly arrived, establishing contact with a familiar adult, whether they are known or not, or achieving a placement with that individual, may reduce the trauma or stress that a child experiences. (It is also important to acknowledge that if contact or placements are established without due regard for the welfare and protection of the child, it could also be harmful). If responses are not timely, there is a possibility that an opportunity to facilitate a placement is lost. We learned that some children become settled in care placements and their relatives become more accepting of this as they identify short-term benefits in the material advantages and educational opportunities that placements can offer. On one level, this is understandable, particularly where families are asylum seeking and exist on very low levels of income, but we feel that it is important for practitioners to be mindful of both the long-term and short-term implications of growing up in care.

In recognition of the need for a timely response, we established due procedures for referrals to the team to minimise the potential for referrals that were inappropriate and to ensure that we could appropriately prioritise our work. For example, with adequate information, we were able to give priority to cases where the children were particularly vulnerable. Over time, we reached a decision that we would only accept referrals for assessment of prospective carers who were over the age of 18. We placed a responsibility on the child's social worker to provide a written account of the detail provided by the child on the adult's full name, contact information, nature of their relationship to the child and the preferred language of the adult. We also required that a copy of the child's initial needs assessment be passed to the team on referral. We built upon this information by discussing the case with the child's social worker, key worker or foster carer, and through reading the relevant case file and/or care plan. The involvement of the additional worker and the assessment process was always explained to the child.

Initiating an assessment depended upon making contact with the adult concerned. This seems an obvious point and it may also sound as though it is a simple task. However, in our experience, it was seldom straightforward and it was a process that needed to be carefully managed. On a practical level, the contact details provided by the child may be indirect or incorrect. In some cases, where no prior contact with the adult had been made either by the child concerned or anyone else with social services, it may be a source of shock or distress to receive a call regarding the newly arrived child. It may be that the adult has had little or no contact with the child or his or her family for some time and given that the child is likely to have left their country due to being at risk of persecution it may also be that the adult has been dealing with a considerable amount of distress or pressure in not knowing anything about the child or their family. In other cases, the adults may already be aware of the child's arrival, having been informed by an agent or someone within the child's support network, and have been in contact with social services or be in expectation of contact from the child. In any event, contact is likely to result in a strong urge to see or collect the child and it may incur strong emotions on the part of the adult when the worker explains that this is not immediately possible. At this juncture, the skill and sensitivity of the worker were crucial. What happens at this point, lays the foundations for the future relationship between the worker and prospective carer. In our view, the quality of a relationship was key to the success of the assessment process; and while we were mindful that we do not know the identity of the adults, we maintained our sensitivity and respect for their needs and concerns as family members participating in a process of assessment.

In our experience, making the initial contact by telephone was better than making contact in writing. It allowed us to work quickly and directly; we knew instantly if a prospective carer had received and understood the information. Telephone interpreters were always used, unless we were certain of an adult's fluency and preference for English. We always identified ourselves by name and provided a direct telephone number, usually, both our office direct dial and mobile numbers, so that the prospective carer could get in touch directly with the kinship care worker. Being available and accessible assisted with the formation of trusting, working relationships with the adults participating in an assessment. For some adults concerned for their child, a clear point of contact represented a lifeline. At the outset, we simply and clearly explained the objectives of the assessment and the process, with an indication of timescales.

At this stage, we always made a firm arrangement to meet as soon as practically possible, taking into consideration geographical distance and travel arrangements and the availability of the family member who is to be assessed as the principal carer. The circumstances on a case-by-case basis dictated whether or not the first meeting took place in the family home, which could be anywhere in the United Kingdom, or at the social work office in Kent. Again, it was important that we were flexible in this and able to travel to meet with the adult or family. It was always made clear that the child would not be present at the initial meeting, as the focus was on the assessment and the possible permanent 'reunification' of the child with the family. The first meeting set the scene for the interaction, and professional relationship, between the practitioner and the family. Consequently, the practitioner must manage it in a way that remains open and flexible to the family. As part of this, it is crucial that the assessment is conducted in the family's first or preferred language and that the participating interpreters are appropriately trained and professional in their work. It is also crucial that the practitioner is able to deal with the emotional context within which they are working – in our experience, we worked with raw emotion in a way that we had never done before and we had to find ways to ensure that the assessment process was not damaging to anyone involved.

A primary focus of a first meeting was to identify how the child and adult were related. The genogram proved to be the most useful tool for this. More than a fact-finding device, it elicited a narrative from the adult or family that also allows for, amongst other things, their exploration of their level of commitment to the child. In the construction of the genogram, a visual diagram of a family tree, 'the family unit is defined and issues of structure and function are illustrated, in addition to displaying factual information such as births, illnesses, deaths, marriages, divorces, occupations, and religious and ethnic affiliations' (Walton and Smith, 1999: 7). Managing this process requires care and sensitivity, as narratives may contain difficult and troubling memories. During the process, the adult's knowledge of the child's past becomes evident and in our experience it is the small details, the minutia of family life, which are significant for the matching of the child and adult as family or kinship members. In some cases, it became apparent that another adult was more appropriate as a carer, which necessitated a change in focus. We also gathered information, with the consent of the family, from other formal agencies (eg., police, social services in their area, asylum or housing services, health services, schools) in the United Kingdom. This not only assisted with building a picture of the family, it provided an insight into the practical resources available to the family and established links that could be used if the child went to live in that area with the family.

To some extent, the need to establish a level of confidence that the child and adult are who they say they are, have a connection to each other (irrespective of whether that is biological or not) prefaces an assessment of the family's capacity to care (although the process necessarily involves being mindful of both objectives). In some cases, we found that it was not possible to establish a match on the basis of the information provided, particularly where truncated family trees were presented alongside seemingly set accounts of their respective stories. Such situations present significant challenges for the practitioner, and, again, the strength and quality of the relationship formed influences the ability to engage the adult and child in an ongoing process of information gathering. However, even where contradictions existed we found it was important to bear in mind that multiple narratives of a family's history could exist. In our experience, it was only in a few cases that it was not possible to establish a connection and the gaps or inconsistencies were extreme enough to suggest that it may not be appropriate to recommend a placement.

In the final stages of the assessment process, we collated all information and provided a written appraisal of the information in the format of a formal report. Reports incorporated current biographical data on the child and main care giver, and narrative detail about the family composition, including the genograms, and an account of the child and adult's current circumstances (specifically health needs, education, implications of immigration status). A crucial part was the risk assessment, where both positive and negative factors were identified. The assessment also identified any resources needed to facilitate the placement or matters that need to be addressed prior to placement, such as legal or medical appointments in a distant geographical area. This process usually involved discussions with the supervisor, or in the team as a whole, where difficulties were explored and solutions discussed. At times, it also included discussions with the child's social worker to explore any actions necessary to resolve practical issues (eg., housing). The kinship social worker's appreciation of potential practical constraints informed the recommendations but this did not determine the outcome of the assessment. The assessment's objective was to address the question of whether or not a kinship placement can safely occur. However, the final decision regarding the placement rested with the child's social worker, and his or her manager, on consideration of the child's needs and the level of support that can be provided by the family and social services.

Outcomes of assessments and placements achieved

Between March 2002, when we received our first referral, and November 2004, when work began for this chapter, we received 154 referrals. The referrals originated from the duty team who were responsible for dealing with referrals of newly arrived children and young people or from the team responsible for supporting them in the long term. The children and young people were in the main under the age of 16, and at the point of the referral 'looked after' by the local authority. The vast majority (83 per cent) of these referrals resulted in an assessment being initiated and completed. An assessment was not initiated or completed for 17 per cent of the referrals for a number of reasons. In some cases, it was apparent early on that a placement was not viable. For example, if the proposed carer was under 18 years of age. In other cases, assessments were not completed if the proposed carers failed to respond or if their circumstances changed unexpectedly. Some adults withdrew from the process after deciding that they did not want to care for the child or to undertake any assessment, and in a small number of cases, it was the child who chose to withdraw. In these cases, it was possible for the assessment process to be re-initiated at anytime.

Of the 128 cases that resulted in a completed assessment, 107 concerned boys and 21 girls. The children ranged in age from six-year olds to seventeen-year olds and although the majority (73 per cent) were aged between 13 and 15 years, a sizeable minority (19 per cent) were aged 12 years or younger. The adults who were assessed presented as a range of relatives, including parent or parents (14 per cent), siblings (19 per cent), aunts or uncles (19 per cent), cousins (34 per cent) or more distant relatives (9 per cent). A small proportion

Table 7.1   Outcome Following Assessment Recommendation

Outcome following assessment	Numbers of assessments	
	Placement recommended	Placement not recommended
Reunified with parent	19	
Moved to live with kin	76	
Contact facilitated		5
Remained in SSD care	9	15
Absconded from care		4
Total	104	24

(6 per cent) of cases involved the assessment of an unrelated adult as a prospective carer.

The complexity of the assessments varied and as a result the time taken to complete them ranged from one day to almost seven months. The average completion time was 46 days. A substantial proportion (38 per cent) of the assessments were completed within one month and the overwhelming majority (74 per cent) within two months of the date of referral to the kinship assessment team. The cases that involved parents required the shortest possible timescale, unless there was evidence of child protection concerns. It is important to bear in mind that if the assessment confirms a parent-child relationship, a child is no longer deemed to be unaccompanied and therefore, in most cases, should not remain 'looked after'. The local authority has no right to provide accommodation for a child if a person with parental responsibility is willing and able to provide or arrange accommodation for them (section 20(7)).

Table 7.1 illustrates the final outcome following the completion of kinship assessments. It shows that occasionally certain children remained in their current placement despite there being a recommendation for them to be placed with the adult assessed. This may be due to changes in the relative's circumstances or in rare cases if the child chooses not to move. It also shows that in some cases it was not appropriate for children to move to live within their kinship networks. All of the placements achieved were subsequently supported under section 17 of the Children Act 1989.

Reflections

The context to our work was perhaps exceptional in the United Kingdom. As we have indicated, Kent was responsible for the arrival of very large numbers of unaccompanied children. This necessitated, as well as justified, the development of a professional role, in the form of four social workers, dedicated to the assessment of friends and family members as potential carers for unaccompanied children. However, there are a number of aspects to our work that were not exclusive to Kent. Law and policy, and some research evidence, indicates that it is potentially positive for children and young people to live with friends or family members where they are not able to live with their parents. Social workers have a duty to work towards this. In the context of working with unaccompanied asylum seeking children, a unique challenge exists as such friends or family members may be unknown to the child and in all cases their connection or inter-related history is undocumented. Existing procedures and assessment models do not allow for this, and social work practitioners are unlikely to have previously encountered situations where this is the case. Furthermore, this lack of certainty is overshadowed by concerns surrounding trafficking, which creates fear and suspicion that may inhibit practice.

In our experience, as a team, we were permitted a level of autonomy that allowed us to be flexible and creative and to make mistakes. In retrospect, it became apparent that the make-up of our team was significant to our development of practice. Our combined experience (drawn from a combined 75 years in practice) and knowledge (derived from our work in children and families' child protection and placements teams) was an asset. We were each able to make sound professional judgements and decisions with confidence and were able to determine when a certain policy should not or could not be followed in a particular instance. As a result of our experience and appreciation of the research, policy and legislative context, we valued the importance of family ties and community networks to the whole continuum of a child's needs and experience. We were able to recognise that narrow conceptualisations of 'family' have a tendency to dominate practice and were able to see these as potentially limiting our perspectives as practitioners. We were willing to continually re-evaluate our individual and professional ideas about family, childrearing and care.

With the benefit of hindsight, we feel our practice originated from a standpoint that focused upon possibility. We asked ourselves why a placement could happen and looked for solutions, rather than focus upon why it could not and become preoccupied by problems. However, if we situated our practice alongside an appraisal of the good practice literature on kinship care (Doolan et al., 2004; Broad and Skinner, 2005) it may appear that it is overly preoccupied with risk and that considerable progress needs to be made before it can be considered as fully collaborative. Nonetheless, we consider it to be a step in the right direction; it is an evolving area of practice, and we feel that we have successfully challenged some of the notions that were inhibiting practice within our authority and which, we know on the basis of anecdotes, inhibit practice in other authorities.

Children and young people's views and wishes were taken into account. Families were able to participate more fully in the decision-making process. We feel we assisted children and young people to live together with their chosen 'family' where it was likely to be safe. We encountered cases where there were indications that it was not likely to be safe in one environment, but negotiated alternatives within the kinship network on the basis of what the group as a whole felt was good for the child. We also encountered cases where it was apparent that it was more appropriate for a child to remain looked after, in order to fulfil the duty to safeguard and promote the welfare of a child in need. The fact that these three different scenarios are possible emphasise the need for a process of assessment. However, our experience suggests that there needs to be more consideration, at a national level, of what is involved in working to assess, as well as support, the friends and family of unaccompanied children as their prospective carers.

References

Broad, B. and Skinner, A. (2005). *Relative Benefits. Placing Children in Kinship Care.* London: BAAF.

Department of Health. (1991). *The Foster Placement (Children) Regulations 1991.* London: HMSO.

——. (1995). *Unaccompanied Asylum Seeking Children. A Practice Guide.* London: Department of Health.

——. (2002). *Fostering Services. National Minimum Standards. Fostering Services Regulations.* London: The Stationery Office.

——. (2003). Guidance on accommodating children in need and their families. Local Authority Circular, 2 June 2003, *LAC*(2003)13. (Available online: http://www.dh.gov.uk/assetRoot/04/01/27/56/04012756.pdf)

Doolan, M., Nixon, P. and Lawrence, P. (2004). *Growing Up in the Care of Relatives or Friends. Delivering Best Practice for Children in Friends and Family Care.* London: Family Rights Group.

Flynn, R. (2000). Kinship foster care, *National Children's Bureau Highlight*, 179.

——. (2002). Research review: Kinship foster care, *Child and Family Social Work*, 7: 311–321.

Gilroy, P. (2001). Away from home, alone, *Community Care*, 2–8 August: 26–27.

Greeff, R., Waterhouse, S. and Brocklesby, E. (1999.) Kinship fostering – Research, policy and practice in England. In R. Greeff (ed.), *Fostering Kinship. An International Perspective on Kinship Foster Care.* Aldershot: Ashgate Publishing.

Hayes, D. (2002). London and the South East bear most of the cost of asylum seeking children, *Community Care*, 31 October – 6 November 2002: 10.

Kidane, S. (2001). *Food, Shelter, and Half a Chance: Assessing the Needs of Unaccompanied Asylum Seeking and Refugee Children.* London: BAAF.

Kohli, R. K. S. (2003). Promoting psychosocial well-being in unaccompanied asylum seeking young people in the United Kingdom, *Child and Family Social Work*, 8 (3): 201–212.

Laming, H. (2003). *The Victoria Climbie Inquiry: Report of an Inquiry by Lord Laming.* London: HMSO.

Philpot, T. (2001). *A Very Private Practice.* London: BAAF.

——. (2003). Bad Company? *Community Care*, 6–12 November, 2003: 34.

Ryburn, M. (1998). A new model of welfare: Re-asssserting the value of kinship for children in state care, *Social Policy and Administration*, 32 (1): 28–45.

Taitz, J., Weekers, J. E. M. and Mosca, D. T. (2002) The last resort: exploring the use of DNA testing for family reunification, *Health and Human Rights*, 6 (1): 21–34.

Somerset, C. (2004). *Cause for Concern? London Social Services and Child Trafficking*. London: ECPAT.

Wade, J., Mitchell, F. and Baylis, G. (2005). *Unaccompanied Asylum Seeking Children: The Response of Social Work Services*. London: BAAF.

Walton, E. and Smith, C. (1999). The Genogram: A tool for assessment, *Journal of Family Social Work*, 3 (3): 3–20.

CHAPTER 8

Using Foster Placements for the Care and Resettlement of Unaccompanied Children

Rachel Hek

Introduction

In 2004, unaccompanied children accounted for five per cent of all 'looked after' children (DfES, 2005). This proportion is likely to increase, as local authorities are likely to 'look after' more unaccompanied children than has previously been the case. In recent years, central government have re-issued statutory guidance reiterating the duty to 'look after' unaccompanied children and the practice of supporting unaccompanied children as children 'in need' has been subject to legal challenge. Bearing this in mind, this chapter explores how foster placements can be used, and supported, to assist unaccompanied children. Relatively little research exists that explores the fostering of unaccompanied children, either from their own perspective or from that of the foster carers supporting them. Therefore, this chapter draws on: literature which documents the foster care experience of looked after children, in general; research which explores the general experiences of unaccompanied children arriving into the United Kingdom; research which has been conducted with unaccompanied children in emergency situations overseas and on social work practice with unaccompanied children in other industrialised nations. In doing so, the chapter explores a number of factors that may contribute to ensuring that foster placements are successful and do assist children and young people to find a sense of stability, security and belonging while in the United Kingdom.

Looked after children's views and experiences of foster care

A few studies have looked at life in foster care from children and young people's perspectives (Fletcher, 1993; Ince, 1998; Andersson, 1999; Heptinstall et al.,

2001; Sinclair et al., 2001). Berridge (1997) emphasises that such studies are important, as children's views and experiences are a key indicator of successful and good quality foster placements. In summary, the research contains a number of key messages for social workers and foster carers. Children and young people

- say they want to feel valued, encouraged and cared for in the same way as other children within the foster home;
- think that there should be choice and options and that they should be able to meet with carers before being placed;
- often rate their foster carers as being highly important people in their lives – for those in longer term placements carers are often rated as more important than birth parents;
- report a sense of 'not belonging' and feeling different. This is heightened by: the number of people involved in their lives, the occurrence of meetings about their lives, differences between their surnames and those of their foster families, and social workers not listening to their views;
- highlight contact as an important issue. Some emphasise how much they wanted contact – with siblings as well as birth parents. Others were clear that they did not want contact, with some or all of their families, and wished social workers would respect this.

There is always a feeling of impermanence with children who are looked after, and consequently it is hard for these young people to feel secure. They say that regular review and planning meetings help so that they know what is going on in their lives. The 'sense' of permanence has been highlighted as more important for children than actual legal permanence.

Ince's (1998) study of the experiences of black care leavers (which looks at residential as well as foster placements) found many of the young people did not feel they received enough input from social workers or carers about their cultural or ethnic identity during their time in placement. Those who had been placed trans-racially questioned this decision, feeling that if they had been placed with black carers this may have been better for them. Most of the young people stated that they were not listened to about what they wanted from their placements. The overall message from children is that placements work best for them when they are consulted at each step by their social workers and other carers to determine what they want.

Foster care for unaccompanied children

As just stated, there is little information specifically about unaccompanied children's views and experiences of fostering, which reflects more generally a limited awareness of their needs and wishes. In studies where unaccompanied children have been asked for their views and experiences of placement on arrival in the United Kingdom, they have highlighted a number of overarching issues in relation to foster care placements that help them settle and minimise emotional difficulties (Kidane, 2001a; Stanley, 2001). They talked about finding somewhere to live that provides safety; where their experiences will be recognised, but they will not be pressurised to talk about them unless they want to; and somewhere that is suitable in terms of language, culture and religion. Research has been undertaken on the fostering of unaccompanied children in emergency situations overseas, and in relation to social work practices in countries such as Sweden, the United States, Canada and Australia. In Africa and South America, Tolfree (2004) found that unaccompanied children expressed a number of strong wishes for: being treated as part of the foster family, for example, getting the same care as others in the family; being placed with their siblings; help with finding a school, settling in and attending regularly; and being helped to find or to stay in contact with family members. In the literature on fostering and social work practice with unaccompanied children, three main topics are considered in relation to fostering as a placement choice for unaccompanied children – the advantages and disadvantages of foster care; cultural issues and fostering; and ways in which placements can be supported.

The advantages and disadvantages of fostering for unaccompanied children

There has been much debate around the advantages and disadvantages of fostering as a placement choice for unaccompanied children, and it is often compared with specialist group care (Mougne, 1985; Zulfacar, 1987; Steinbock, 1996; Tolfree, 2004). Guidelines issued by the United Nations High Commission for Refugees (UNHCR, 1994) regarding the protection and care of refugee children refer to the placement needs of unaccompanied children. It stresses the importance of continuous, loving and nurturing care. The UNHCR (1994) suggests that the intention should be to place these children in 'the context of the family and the community' (2), as this is more likely to attend to their developmental and cultural needs. The document states that: 'Every effort must be made to place children in foster families or groups of similar ethnic, cultural, linguistic and religious background' (UNHCR, 1994, article 20). It also recognises that each child will have different placement needs and that for some children family care will be the best option whilst for others group care may be more appropriate.

Drawing on findings from the United States, Germany and Australia, Zulfacar (1987) summarises some advantages and disadvantages of fostering for unaccompanied children. He makes the point that some of this material has not been rigorously researched and is often based on anecdotal evidence. Much of the evidence discussed relates to trans-racial and trans-cultural foster placements, where it is suggested that the specific experiences, cultural and religious needs of unaccompanied children, have not been recognised in the same way as in specialist group homes. There is little evidence available in relation to ethnically similar foster placements. The advantages of foster care include:

- The provision of individual care and support, which may be particularly helpful emotionally to a young person.
- A quicker adjustment to the new language and system.
- The degree of stability and ongoing care it can provide, particularly, if family reunion does not take place. For example, once a young person leaves the care system they may keep links with the foster carers.
- The potential to assist a young person to make the transition back to the care of their family if reunion does take place. It is thought that the experience of being temporarily looked after in a family situation may mean that less adjustment is required, than if they have been looked after in group-care.

However, some of these points are closely related to what have been identified as the disadvantages of foster care. The experience of being suddenly in the midst of a different family may be overpowering for some young people, even if backgrounds of the young person and carers are similar. The potentially intense nature of this experience may make it more difficult to gradually adjust to the new culture and system. Fostering can be isolating and does not necessarily provide opportunities for peer group interaction, which diminishes the possibility of sharing common experiences and problems. Foster carers may not have the same levels of specialist knowledge in relation to resettlement and adjustment that specialist group care can offer. Fostering does not necessarily provide specific cultural input and familiarity, or allow for language and identity maintenance in the same way that specialist group care can. Such care may be provided by workers with particular skills, from a variety of cultural backgrounds, and there may be other young people in placement from the same ethnic or cultural background. Building 'new' family ties in a fostering situation may undermine 'old' family ties more than placement in a non-family situation, and therefore fostering may place the young person in a position where they feel that their loyalties are split between their own families and their foster families.

Other studies back up Zulfacar's findings. Linowitz and Boothby (1988) suggest that foster care may cause particular difficulties for children in relation to feelings of guilt when they compare their new situation to the family they may feel they have 'left behind'. Jockenhövel-Schiecke (1990) states that unaccompanied children often clash with foster carers who try to assume a parental role, when they are coming to terms with feelings of loss and guilt in relation to their own family. Tolfree (2004) summarised a number of studies of fostering initiated by the International Save the Children Alliance in Africa and South America. He states that the studies found that there was a common perception amongst children of being 'different' because they were fostered and some confusion and ambivalence about 'family' relationships. Some children also talked about the need to 'behave better' and achieve more than other children in the family, in a bid to gain acceptance. They also expressed different understandings of what being fostered meant to them; this was often based on how permanently they viewed the arrangement. Where they saw the fostering arrangement as permanent, they were more able to feel settled and consider their future.

Cultural issues and fostering

Fostering may be a confusing or unknown concept to many unaccompanied children. In many cultures there may be a tradition of living with or being cared for by family or friends but little concept of living with strangers; children's understandings of being fostered are culturally shaped (Tolfree, 2004). This is illustrated by the findings of a number of case studies that have been carried out with children and those who had become foster carers in emergency situations in Tanzania, Democratic Republic of Congo, Rwanda, Malawi and El Salvador (Mann and Tolfree, 2003). The studies found that the idea of being fostered had strong negative connotations for many children (Tolfree, 2004). Children assumed they would be treated in a discriminatory and abusive manner if placed in 'foster families'. They talked about being used as 'slaves', not being allowed to attend school and being treated less favourably than foster carers' own children. These and other studies (Phiri and Duncan, 1993) found that the fear of abuse, discrimination and exploitation in emergency situations is based in reality as this does take place in some foster placements. This may have implications for the perceptions of unaccompanied children and young people who find themselves placed with foster carers upon arrival in the United Kingdom, despite the fact that many children will receive good and protective care.

Linowitz and Boothby (1988) argue that it is important to consider culture in placement choice, as it is a major factor in the successful resettlement of unaccompanied children. These authors bring together a range of research findings from studies, carried out in the United States, Australia, France and the Netherlands, which compare the outcomes for unaccompanied children looked after in trans-racial and trans-cultural situations and those placed with carers from an ethnically similar background. The studies they consider suggest that ethnically similar placements seem to promote more positive emotional experiences, particularly during the early resettlement period for children, and may even result in lower rates of depression. However, there was little difference found in the ability to adjust and integrate (ie., learn English, make progress in school, make friends) between those young people placed with ethnically similar carers and those trans-racially placed. Zulfacar (1987) found a suggestion that ethnically matched placements are less likely to break down, and may provide some similarities with the home backgrounds of young refugees. However, Linowitz and Boothby (1988) also present a more complex picture of the benefits and disadvantages of placement with families who are themselves from refugee backgrounds. It suggests that some children may be slower to adjust to their new situation because refugee carers may not have the same level of understanding of or access to the system as indigenous carers.

Young refugees often have their own views about where they feel they would be best placed, and their social background and individual circumstances pre-exile will play a part in this. Some children said that being with a family or other children from their own cultural background was helpful (Kidane, 2001b), whilst others said that they preferred to be with English carers as they felt this would speed up their familiarisation with the language and system (Stanley, 2001). Yaya (1998) argues that some children are reluctant to be placed with carers from their country of origin, as they fear that information may be passed on and this may affect the families they have left behind. Although the issue of placement, and 'matching' in particular, is extremely complex, it is most important to consider the views and wishes of young refugees themselves, rather than having a 'blanket' approach, or strict agency position. Individual experiences, needs and preferences all play an important part and flexibility on the part of agencies is crucial. This is an area that would clearly benefit from further research.

Supporting foster placements for unaccompanied children

Given these findings, it is important that foster carers are recruited from as diverse a community as possible if the widest range of options is to be available. Research in relation to recruitment of black and minority ethnic carers, including those from refugee backgrounds, is sparse. However, Tolfree (2004) points to certain factors that may be helpful to understand. Fostering may be culturally unfamiliar (children living with strangers may not be something that would usually occur), and agency criteria for becoming a carer may be daunting. For example, agency expectations of particular types of child-care practice may seem unsettling and baffling and the fostering assessment may be found to be intrusive. He also suggests that carers have different reasons and motivations for becoming involved in fostering. Some referred to religious reasons, such as considering looking after a child as a way of serving God; some felt a humanitarian obligation and some wanted a child if they had lost their own child. These motivations can be important for social workers to understand in order to offer support to carers. A number of strategies have been successful in recruiting carers for young refugees in Malawi and Rwanda. These included government-backed media campaigns; working through community-based organisations and respected local people to promote fostering; working with faith-based organisations to build on people's existing values and promote the idea of fostering as a humanitarian activity; using carers to recruit other carers and finally using children to identify suitable carers within their networks.

Support is a major factor in the success of both trans-racial and ethnically similar foster placements. Linowitz and Boothby (1988) highlight supportive practices, which militate against placement breakdown for unaccompanied children:

- Placement of children in 'clusters', so that they are able to have contact with other children of a similar background.
- Assessment of carers that emphasise their ability to be open and flexible.
- Social workers who provide practical and emotional input for children and carers, and who are available and attentive.
- Facilitation of discussions about differences in cultural expectations and practices for both carers and children can be helpful in avoiding misunderstandings, particularly if the conversation is about 'how are we the same, how are we different, and how can sameness and difference be put to best use for us in living together' and is conducted in the presence of someone whom both parties respect.
- Regular visits from social workers with a worker who is bilingual, speaking the first language of the child can be important in enhancing communication, preventing misunderstanding and reducing isolation. The importance of a bilingual adult in promoting early resettlement is supported by studies in the United Kingdom where children talk about what has helped them to resettle into school and general life (Rutter, 2003; Hek, 2005).

Kidane and Amarena (2004) suggest that help and assistance is also needed by foster carers, as there are particular stresses involved in caring for unaccompanied children; such as hearing stories of violence and trauma, helping children cope with deep feelings of loss and abandonment, understanding behaviour that may result from their experiences. They suggest that training and the chance to discuss issues with a social worker they trust helps this process. Tolfree (2004) highlights the importance of agency monitoring and advice for carers, as he found that many carers felt isolated and lonely. He suggests that work can be carried on in this direction so that fostering is seen as usual and recognised as an alternative family form within local communities. He feels that this not only provides direct support to the carer and young person, but also provides important safeguards and protection. This is borne out in the United Kingdom in the research on what makes foster care safer. Boushel (1994) and Nixon (2000) suggest that if carers are able to engage in discussions with other parents in their local community and professionals in an 'ordinary' way about the stresses and benefits of parenting, then this can help combat feelings of isolation and allow for openness about difficulties they may be experiencing. These types of candid discussions will in turn promote safer care.

Implications for practice: key aspects of the foster care task

There is a wealth of guidance and literature, with respect to foster children, which has relevance to supporting unaccompanied children in foster placements, and beyond. In being attentive to this literature, while also being mindful of the specific circumstances of unaccompanied children, social workers and foster carers, in partnership, can assist them to make a successful transition to life in the United Kingdom and to develop during the time that they are here (whether that is a temporary or permanent period in their lives). The following sections explore some aspects of support that connect to the particular circumstances of unaccompanied children.

Developing a sense of stability

Children and young people who have participated in research studies have reported that they value practical assistance, and have emphasised the types of assistance that have mattered the most to them when they first arrived into the country (Stanley, 2001). They have talked about how important it was to find a placement where they were welcomed; a reliable legal representative who could speedily deal with their application for asylum and someone who could assist them with developing their language skills, settling into school or college, and accessing health services.

What is experienced as welcoming in a placement is not made explicit in the literature. However, in the appraisal of the fostering literature, whether or not a placement is ethnically or culturally similar to a young person's background, it is clear that cultural sensitivity or competency can contribute to whether a placement is experienced as welcoming. Being given access to familiar foods, the chance to talk (or not to talk) about how they are feeling both physically or emotionally, to be able to explore with them the meaning of race, culture, religion and class are all factors that can help children settle into a placement (Stanley, 2001); as are experiences of being cared for and protected, of feeling emotional warmth and stimulation, being given guidance and boundaries, and of developing a sense of stability and security. This latter point connects closely to the impact of the asylum seeking process on the lives of unaccompanied children.

Immigration status for young refugees is 'an issue that permeates all other aspects of their lives' (Mynott and Humphries, 2003: 24). In light of this, it is not surprising that young people identify the outcome of their application as key to their sense of being able to resettle and a major factor in how happy and secure they feel (Stone, 2000; Stanley, 2001). Therefore, it is likely to be significant to a young person where carers and social workers are sensitive to this and assist with ensuring that a young person is receiving good quality service from a legal representative; is kept up-to-date with the progress of his or her application; and is accompanied to formal meetings regarding his or her immigration status by someone who is well informed and able to support them.

Refugee children have also reported that education is extremely important to them (Candappa and Ehharevba, 2000; Kidane, 2001b; Hek, 2005). Attending school or college as soon as possible after being placed can assist children and young people to gain a sense of stability. Foster carers can aid this process by assisting them to settle into school or college life. In doing so, carers want to explore how a school or college welcomes and supports refugee children by asking if it

- values their contribution;
- has classroom support to assist refugee children with settling in and lan guage acquisition;
- promotes opportunities for children to take lessons or sit exams in their first language;
- ensures there are good links with a child's home, so that carers can be kept informed as to what is going on for the child;
- deals effectively with racism and discrimination

With regard to the last point, research and policy literature has emphasised the importance of an ethos of inclusion and respect; anti-bullying policies and the effective monitoring and application of sanctions against bullying and racism; an inclusive and diverse curriculum; working with community agencies to challenge bullying and racism outside of school (Richman, 1998a; Rutter, 2003).

Promoting health and emotional well-being

There are a number of factors that social workers and foster carers may need to be mindful of in their promotion of the health and emotional well-being of unaccompanied children. In fulfilling the statutory requirements of medical, dental and optical checks for foster children, appointments and check-ups may need to be carried out with sensitivity and unaccompanied children supported through out the process. Some may have little experience of routine health care pre-exile or such checking may be associated with repression in their home country (Burnett and Peel, 2001). Additionally, there may be particular issues affecting children from particular regions, for example, female genital mutilation or HIV/AIDS, which require specialist medical skills or attention. Many health trusts now have guidelines and procedures in relation to the health needs of young refugees (Camden Education and Camden and Islington Health Authority, 1999). These can be useful as they may address some of the issues relating to particular communities in the area, and can help professionals think about relevant issues when planning and delivering local services.

There has been some considerable discussion about the potential and varying affects of pre- and post-exile experiences on the mental health of unaccompanied children (Woodcock, 1994; Levenson and Sharma, 1999; Stanley,
2001). Although some refugee children will experience serious, sometimes
prolonged emotional difficulties and may require specialist treatment, this is
not the case for all refugee children (Richman, 1998b). Unaccompanied children may not be open to sharing their experiences or feelings. They may find it
hard to talk about the past, and can appear to be secretive, silent and mistrustful. They may have been told not to give out information about their age,
where their family are or even who they are. They may have been told that this
information will put them or their family in danger, or have an influence on
what will happen to them (Melzak, 1999; Kidane and Amarena, 2004).
Although this type of secretive or withdrawn behaviour may be familiar to
experienced foster carers, who have looked after other vulnerable children
(Beek and Schofield, 2004), there are likely to be differences. For example,
carers for indigenous children are used to having access to some sort of history
and background for the children they look after, often provided by the social
workers. In the case of unaccompanied young refugees it is unlikely that anyone will have this information but the child themselves. This can make it difficult for social workers or foster carers to support them.

Simmonds (2004) observes that children may have confused and contradictory feelings about why their parents or family sent them away; they may have
been told it was to keep them safe, but have experienced feelings of abandonment or rejection. He also suggests that they may find it difficult to give a
coherent story as their experiences of the journey to foster care is likely to have
been frightening, fragmented and incoherent. Kohli (2006) also talks about
incoherent stories and the use of silence by unaccompanied children. He suggests that as well as being an indication of psychological trauma, silence can
also serve a protective function that allows young people to get on with the
'here and now' aspects of their lives. He sees social workers as having an
important role to play as 'trusted companions over time' (12) and 'therapeutically minded listeners' (14) who are able to live with either silence or stories
that change over time, thereby allowing young people to feel safe and to use
emotional support at their own pace and in their own ways.

Social workers and foster carers are often well placed to provide emotional
support in a non-stigmatising way. Therapy and counselling may not be something refugee children have any experience or knowledge of, and it may not be
usual to discuss personal feelings with people outside of the family
(Summerfield, 1998). It is important that their distress is recognised as being
'a normative and adaptive communication' (424). Concepts and questions
developed through clinical psychotherapeutic work with young refugees can
provide a useful framework for social work practitioners to consider when providing emotional support or counselling. Melzak (1999) and Woodcock
(1994) both suggest that levels of intellectual and emotional development
should be considered, as well as experiences of oppression, violence and

discrimination that have been faced. They also suggest thinking of the losses, trauma and changes children have experienced, whilst not assuming that emotional distress will take the same form or will be about the same issues for all children. This allows practitioners to ensure that each young person is viewed as an individual who is likely to have some experiences that are similar to others and some that are different. It can build on strengths and engage young people in a discussion of what they think they need, whilst not ignoring the emotional aspects of the loss of home. Some may wish to participate in therapy or counselling (Richman, 1998b; Gosling, 2000; Marriott, 2001; Stanley, 2001).

Research studies suggest that input should be holistic and will be most useful if it is practical, educational and social, bolstering their resilience rather than playing on vulnerabilities and discussing painful experiences directly (Bolloten and Spafford, 1998; Richman, 1998). Gilligan (1999) points to the ways in which children can be helped to bolster and maximise the capabilities that they already have, through encouraging their participation in chosen activities. By allowing children to find culturally meaningful and safe ways to process feelings and to recognise that experiences and circumstances are different for individuals, Kohli and Mather (2003:.207) suggest 'feelings of disconnection between past, present and future' will be lessened and this can assist children in beginning to ask for help.

Building relationships and facilitating contact

The building of new formal and informal networks is an integral part of settling into a new community – it comes with any move that people make, whether local, national or international. For unaccompanied children, with few, if any, existing links in the United Kingdom, the support of social workers and foster carers in assisting them to make links, build relationships and become an integral part of different communities is key. Therefore, the relationships that develop between unaccompanied child and social worker, foster child and foster carer will have an influence on the capacity for such networks to develop. For example, it is more likely for unaccompanied children to trust social workers or foster carers where they have had positive experiences, feel cared for and are known by both. Social workers and carers can build up trust through consistent relationships.

In the early days, it may be that young people experience consistency in the practical and emotional support that is provided to them as they adapt to new situations, such as learning a new language, making new friends, going to school, and so on (Gilligan, 1999). With reference to social workers, it might be experienced if they are in regular contact with their social workers, if they are honest about what they can and cannot do, and are included in making plans (Kidane, 2001b). With reference to foster care, young people have indicated that the most helpful thing about foster care is feeling liked, valued and cared for. The experience is negative when they feel isolated, uncared for and when they are treated differently and not included in the carer's network (Kidane, 2001b). It may be helpful for unaccompanied children if carers are able to recognise the impact of major losses of family and home, the experience of finding oneself in another culture and system and feelings of exclusion through racism experienced in the United Kingdom. An important task for the social worker in this situation may be to support the carer by giving information, or by accessing specific training for the carer in relation to issues affecting unaccompanied young refugees (Kidane and Amarena, 2004). It is also likely to be important for social workers to provide similar opportunities to others in the carer's own network, so they can also gain understanding of the needs of the young person and of ways to help them (Tolfree, 2004).

If the foundation for relationships with social workers and foster carers is strong, it may assist young people to talk more openly about their feelings in relation to loss and separation. Unaccompanied children may have experienced prolonged periods away from their families, the death of parents or other close relatives, and they may have little or no knowledge of their families. Family tracing can be attempted through the Red Cross or International Social Services (as this can be dangerous for parents/family members or the child they check whether safety will be compromised). Social workers may have to deal with the emotional repercussions of this. Careful planning, avoiding raising hopes and providing ongoing emotional support have all been found to be helpful (Bonnerjea, 1994; DoH, 1995; Kidane, 2001a). Painful issues may arise as children begin to talk about the loss of home and family. Blackwell (1997) argues that the job of social workers at such a time is not to become caught up in 'doing things', but listen to what the child is saying or 'to bear witness' (81). Blackwell and Melzac (2000) also talk about the importance of workers providing an environment where children feel 'held' (looked after and cared about) and 'contained' (have a feeling that their behaviour will be managed). Reunion can also raise difficult feelings as both children and parents may have changed since they were last together. Emotions such as guilt, anger and feelings of intense disappointment can arise and again listening and providing a space to explore these emotions may be of use (DoH, 1995; Kidane, 2001a).

Mann (2001) states that when children have been through dangerous and stress inducing situations talking with other children who understand this can be preventative to the development of serious emotional difficulties. Children talk about the importance of their friends in many contexts, such as at school, outside of school and in their own communities. Stanley (2001) found that many young refugees gained enormous benefits from spending time with refugee peers, and indicated the importance of informal friendship networks. Young people talked about the importance of maintaining links with refugee communities and taking part in social activities outside of their living situation. They found this helped them feel happier and less isolated.

Conclusion

The studies considered in this chapter suggest that there are a number of ways that foster placements can be used to care for and help unaccompanied young people re-settle in the United Kingdom, and although the literature and research about how fostering is experienced and can help unaccompanied young people is patchy and often advocacy-based, there are some emerging messages that can usefully inform practice in this area.

Unaccompanied children have multifaceted understandings of and responses to the fostering experience, which can be informed by their pre-exile experiences and cultural understandings of fostering. In order to try and understand such meanings this helping process is most useful if it is informed by recognising each young person as an individual with both different and similar experiences to others. It is likely that whatever be the reason a child has been forced to leave home and family, s/he will have experienced feelings of loss, insecurity and isolation. Social workers and foster carers can work together with children to re-build feelings of security and where necessary feelings of confidence and self-worth. Gilligan (2004) sees relationships with key people and the sense of having a 'secure base' in the world as providing a sense of belonging. For unaccompanied young people who do not have this secure base in the United Kingdom, a web of support can be woven around them to provide some of what they are likely to have lost. This may be through social, educational, recreational or professional helping relationships and through practical and emotional assistance. This chapter highlights the need for more in-depth research about how fostering can be used to help and how it is experienced by unaccompanied children and young people. It also suggests that relationships with social workers and carers are key to helping children avoid serious emotional difficulties, to develop new connections, networks and to move forward and re-settle.

References

Andersson, G. (1999). Children in permanent foster care in Sweden, *Child and Family Social Work*, 4: 175–186.

Beek, M. and Schofield, G. (2004). *Providing a Secure Base in Long-term Foster Care*. London: BAAF.

Berridge, D. (1997). *Foster Care: A Research Review*. London: HMSO.

Blackwell, D. (1997.) Holding, containing and bearing witness: the problem of helpfulness in encounters with torture survivors, *Journal of Social Work Practice*, 11 (2): 81–89.

Blackwell, D. and Melzak, S. (2000). *Far from the Battle but Still at War. Troubled Refugee Children in School*. London: The Child Psychotherapy Trust.

Bolloten, B. and Spafford, T. (1998). Supporting refugee children in East London primary schools'. In J. Rutter and C. Jones (eds), *Refugee Education. Mapping the Field*. Wiltshire: Trentham Books.

Bonnerjea, L. (1994). *Family Tracing: A Good Practice Guide*. London: Save the Children.

Boushel, M. (1994). Keeping safe: strengthening the protective environment of children in foster care, *Adoption and Fostering*, 18 (1): 33–39.

Brown, F. (1987). Counselling Vietnamese refugees: the new challenge, *International Journal for the Advancement of Counselling*, 10 (4): 259–268.

Burnett, A. (2002). *Guide to Health Workers Providing Care for Asylum Seekers and Refugees*. London: Medical Foundation.

Burnett, A. and Peel, M. (2001). Health needs of asylum seekers and Refugees, *British Medical Journal*, 322: 544–547.

Camden Education and Camden and Islington Health Authority. (1999). *Meeting the Needs of Refugee Children: A Checklist for all Staff who Work with Refugee Children in Schools*. London: Camden Education and Camden and Islington Health Authority.

Candappa, M. and Egharevba, I. (2000). 'Extraordinary Childhoods': the social lives of refugee children, *Children 5–16 Research Briefing Number 5*, Economic and Social Research Council. (Available online: http://www.hull.ac.uk/children5to16programme/ briefings/candappa.pdf).

Department of Health. (1995). *Unaccompanied Asylum Seeking Children. A Practice Guide*. London: DOH and Social Services Inspectorate.

DfES. (2004). Children in need in England: Results of a survey of activity and expenditure as reported by Local Authority Social Services' Children and Families Teams for a survey week in February 2003. DfES, Issue Nov. web 01–2004.

——. (2005). Statistics of Education: Children Looked After in England: 2003–2004. London: DfES.

Fletcher, B. (1993). *Not Just a Name – The Views of Young People in Foster and Residential Care*. London: National Consumer Council/ Who Cares? Trust.

Gilligan, R. (1999). Enhancing the resilience of children and young people in public care by mentoring their talents and interests, *Child and Family Social Work*, 4: 187–196.

——. (2004). Promoting resilience in child and family social work: issues for social work practice, education and policy, *Social Work Education*, 23 (1): 93–104.

Gosling, R. (2000). *The Needs of Young Refugees in Lambeth, Southwark and Lewisham*. London: Community Health South London NHS Trust.

Harris, M. J. and Openheimer, D. (2000). *Into the Arms of Strangers. Stories of the Kindertransport*. London: Bloomsbury.

Hek, R. (2005). The role of education in the settlement of young refugees in the U.K: The Experiences of Young Refugees, *Practice*, 17: 3.

Hek, R. and Sales, R. (2002). *Supporting Refugee and Asylum Seeking Children: An Examination of Support Structures in Schools and the Community*. London: Middlesex University, Haringey and Islington Education Departments.

Heptinstall, E., Bhopal, K. and Brannen, J. (2001). Adjusting to a foster family: children's perspectives, *Adoption and Fostering*, 25 (4): 6–16.

Home Office. (2004). *Asylum Statistics: United Kingdom 2003*, 2nd edn. (Available online: http:/homeoffice.gov.uk/rds).

Humphries, B. and Mynott, E. (2001). *Living Your Life across Boundaries; Young Separated Refugees in Greater Manchester*. Manchester: Save the Children.

Ince, L. (1998). *Making it Alone: A study of the Care Experiences of Young Black People*. London: BAAF.

Jockenhövel-Schiecke, H. (ed.) (1990). *Unaccompanied Refugee Children in Europe: Experience with Protection, Placement and Education*. Frankfurt: International Social Service, German Branch.

Kidane, S. (2001a). *Food, Shelter and Half a Chance. Assessing the Needs of Unaccompanied Asylum Seeking and Refugee Children.* London: BAAF.

——. (2001b). *I Did Not Choose to Come Here. Listening to Refugee Children.* London: BAAF.

Kidane, S. and Amarena, P. (2004). *Fostering Unaccompanied Asylum Seeking and Refugee Children. A Training Course for Foster Carers.* London: BAAF.

Kohli, R. K. S. (2006). The sound of silence: listening to what unaccompanied asylum seeking children say and do not say, *British Journal of Social* Work, 36: 707–721.

Kohli, R. K. S. and Mather, R. (2003). Promoting psychosocial well-being in unaccompanied asylum seeking people in the United Kingdom, *Child and Family Social Work*, 8 (3): 201–212.

Levenson, R. and Sharma, A. (1999). *The Health of Refugee Children. Guidelines for Paediatricians.* London: Royal College of Paediatrics and Child Health.

Linowitz, J. and Boothby, N. (1988). Cross-cultural placements. In E. M. Ressler, N. Boothby and D. J. Steinbock (eds), *Unaccompanied Children: Care and Protection in Wars, Natural Disasters and Refugee Movements.* New York: Oxford University Press.

Lynch, M. A. and Cuninghame, C. (2000). Understanding the needs of young asylum seekers, *Archives of Diseases in Childhood*, 83: 384–387.

Mann, G. (2001). *Networks of Support: A Literature Review of Care Issues for Separated Children. A CPSC Case Study.* Stockholm: Save the Children Sweden.

Mann, G. and Tolfree, D. (2003). *Children's Participation in Research: Reflections from the Care and Protection of Separated Children in Emergencies Project. A CPSC Case Study.* Stockholm: Save the Children Sweden.

Marriott, K. (2001). *Living in Limbo; Young Separated Refugees in the West Midlands.* London: Save the Children.

Melzac, S. (1999). Work with refugees from political violence. In M. Lanyado and A. Horne (eds), *The Handbook of Child and Adolescent psychotherapy.* London: Routledge.

Mougne, C. (1985). *Vietnamese Children's Homes: A Special Case for Care?* London: Save the Children.

Mynott, E. and Humphries, B. (2003). Young separated refugees, UK practice and Europeanisation, *Social Work in Europe*, 9 (1): 18–26.

Nixon, S. (2000). Safe care, abuse and allegations of abuse in foster care. In G. Kelly and R. Gilligan (eds), *Issues in Foster Care: Policy, Practice and Research.* London: Jessica Kingsley.

Phiri, S. and Duncan, J. (1993). Substitute family placements of unaccompanied Mozambican children: a field perspective, *Journal of Social Development in Africa*, 8 (2): 73–82.

Richman, N. (1998a). *In the Midst of the Whirlwind. A Manual for Helping Refugee Children.* London: Save the Children.

——. (1998b). Looking before and after: refugees and asylum seekers in the West. In P. J. Bracken and C. Petty (eds), *Rethinking the Trauma of War.* London: Save the Children.

——. (2003). *Working with Refugee Children.* York: Joseph Rowntree Foundation.

Simmonds, J. (2004). Primitive forces in society – how do we hold unaccompanied children in mind? *Adoption and Fostering*, 28(2): 68–75.

Stanley, K. (2001). *Cold comfort. Young Separated Refugees in England.* London: Save the Children.

Steinbock, D. J. (1996). Unaccompanied refugee children in host country foster families, *International Journal of Refugee Law*, 8 (1/2): 6–48.

Stone, R. (2000). *Children first and Foremost. Meeting the Needs of Unaccompanied Asylum Seeking Children*. London: Barnardos.

Summerfield, D. (1998). The social experience of war and some issues for the Humanitarian Field. In P. J. Bracken and C. Petty (eds), *Rethinking the Trauma of War*. London: Save the Children.

Sinclair, D., Wilson, K. and Gibbs, I. (2001). A life more ordinary: what children want from foster placements, *Adoption and Fostering*, 25 (4): 17–26.

Tolfree, D. (2004). *Whose Children? Separated Children's Protection and Participation in Emergencies*. Stockholm: Save the Children Sweden.

UNHCR. (1994). *Refugee Children. Guidelines for Protection and Care*. Geneva: UNHCR.

Woodcock, J. (1994). Family therapy with refugees and political exiles, *Context*, 20: 37–41.

Yaya, B. (1998). Finding substitute carers for unaccompanied refugee children: the European Dimension, *Social Work in Europe*, 3 (3): 49–51.

Zulfacar, D. (1987). Alternative forms of care for unaccompanied refugee minors: a comparison of US and Australian experience, *International Social Work*, 30: 61–75.

CHAPTER 9

Leaving 'Care'? Transition Planning and Support for Unaccompanied Young People

Jo Dixon and Jim Wade

Introduction

Most unaccompanied asylum seeking children and young people come to the United Kingdom in their mid-teen years. In 2004, Home Office statistics suggested that 2990 unaccompanied children made applications for asylum. Of these, 62 per cent were made by young people aged 16 or 17, a further 28 per cent by young people aged 14 or 15 and only 10 per cent of applications were lodged by young people below the age of 14 (Heath and Jeffries, 2005). Given this age profile, preparation and planning for the transition to adulthood should be a central feature of social work practice with unaccompanied young people from the point they first come to the attention of social services. The timescales available for doing so are often relatively short, in many instances only one or two years.

Planning for the future is inevitably crowded by the practical and emotional demands of the present. Young people invariably arrive in a confused and emotional state. While their particular experiences may be divergent, they all carry with them (to varying degrees) the emotional consequences of their ruptured links with family, friends and community, and share a need to find their way in an unfamiliar social landscape. Their primary needs are for settlement – to find peace and stability, an opportunity to build new attachments, to begin or resume education or training and to construct new networks of social support. As we shall see later, these are also important features of preparation for adulthood and for successful transition at a later stage.

Leaving care practice with unaccompanied young people is a challenging area of work, one that is also profoundly influenced by the asylum process. In the context of an increasingly harsh political climate towards asylum seekers in general, the approach of adulthood frequently creates anxiety and further uncertainty for young people. Unaccompanied young people are only rarely granted 'indefinite leave' to remain (ILR) or 'humanitarian protection' (HP) and the majority are given 'discretionary leave' to remain (DL), most often up to their eighteenth birthday. Current signals from government will do little to allay these fears; they point to a future hardening of the stance on returning unaccompanied young people at 18 (or before if adequate reception arrangements exist) and suggest, on receipt of a final negative asylum decision, that social services responsibilities will end (Children's Legal Centre, 2005; Save the Children, 2005; Home Office, 2007).

From a research perspective, studies that explore how social services manage their responsibilities to unaccompanied children have only just started to emerge (Mitchell, 2003). In consequence, we have understood little about how young people negotiate these transitions, how social workers and allied professionals help young people to prepare and plan for their futures nor about how these experiences may compare to those of other care leavers, about whom much more is known. In contributing to this work, this chapter will draw on findings from a recent study (to be known as the York study) that has investigated social work services for unaccompanied children (Wade et al., 2005). It will also situate these findings in the context of broader research knowledge about leaving care and of the relatively new responsibilities given to local authorities by the Children (Leaving Care) Act 2000.

The study design

The purpose of the York study was to assess how social services responded to the needs of unaccompanied children and young people, how their needs were assessed, what services flowed from this assessment, how these services varied for different sub-groups within the population and with what effects for young people's lives and progress. The study was conducted in three local authorities and the sample was selected from all cases of unaccompanied children referred between 1 March 2001 and 31 August 2002. A stratified random sample of 212 young people was selected to ensure a good cross section of cases, taking account of age, sex and length of time since referral (see Wade et al., 2005 for further details). The main fieldwork was undertaken in 2002–2003. A retrospective analysis of social work case files was undertaken for the whole sample and this was complemented by semi-structured interviews with 31 of these young people and their main support workers.

The characteristics of the final sample reflected this sampling strategy – 80 per cent were male and just over half (56 per cent) were aged 16 or 17 at referral, the majority being 14–17 years old (89 per cent). The young people came to the United Kingdom from a total of 23 different countries. Consistent with earlier findings on support for unaccompanied children (Stone, 2000; Stanley, 2001), the majority (76 per cent) were supported under community provisions of the Children Act 1989 (s17) and only a minority (n = 38) were formally looked after.

Law, policy and leaving care pathways

Longstanding concerns about the difficulties faced by citizen young people leaving care have prompted legislative change and the development of specialist leaving care services. These developments form part of the context for thinking about transitions made by unaccompanied young people. Despite their disadvantaged backgrounds, young people have left care at a much earlier age than their peers have left the family home (Biehal et al., 1992; Garnett, 1992; Jones, 1995). Not only do they leave early, but the main elements of transition have also tended to be compressed. Learning to manage a home, start a career and a family have tended to overlap in the period after leaving care (Biehal et al., 1995; Stein, 2004). While some young people fared quite well, others struggled and evidence has consistently pointed to young people facing a heightened risk of unemployment and homelessness (Cheung and Heath, 1994; Broad, 1998) and of social isolation as support from families often proved inconsistent and professional support tended to fall away soon after leaving care (Garnett, 1992; Biehal and Wade, 1996; Marsh and Peel, 1999).

During the 1980s, the emergence of specialist leaving care services represented an important response to these problems. The gradual development of services led to improvements in support and outcomes for young people leaving care, especially in relation to accommodation, financial support and life skills (Biehal et al., 1995). However, these developments were uneven and marked variations in service provision existed between local authorities (Broad, 1998; Stein and Wade 2000). The Children (Leaving Care) Act (CLCA) 2000 was intended to tackle these inconsistencies through new duties to assess and meet the needs of 'eligible' young people and through new arrangements for financial support, pathway planning and provision of personal advisers to guide young people through transition to age 21 or beyond (Department of Health, 2001). Early evidence on implementation of the CLCA suggests that it is prompting some improvements in consistency, planning and support for young people leaving care, although uneven patterns of service delivery persist (Broad, 2003; Hai and Williams, 2004).

For unaccompanied young people, transition pathways at age 18 vary according to both asylum status and the support arrangements previously provided by social services. Where they have been looked after (s20), all duties connected with preparation, pathway planning and after care support apply in the same way as for citizen young people. If young people are still seeking an asylum decision at 18, they are not at risk of dispersal, may continue to study and have the same support entitlements as other care leavers. As things presently stand, they are covered by the provisions of the CLCA until they receive a final negative asylum decision, all appeal rights have been exhausted and they refuse to comply with Home Office removal directions (Children's Legal Centre, 2004; Home Office 2004).

However, the majority of unaccompanied young people have not been protected by this legislation, as they have been supported under section 17 of the Children Act 1989. Local authorities have fewer legal duties with respect to them and no specific duty to provide leaving care services beyond 18. Where young people at age 18 have leave to remain (ILR, HP or DL) or have made an 'in time' application to extend their leave, they have the same social rights (for work, study and housing) as other young people. Where they are seeking asylum at age 18 or have an outstanding appeal, they are likely to transfer to the National Asylum Support Service (NASS), may face dispersal to another area, but may continue to study. Where they have received a final negative decision and exhausted all appeal rights at age 18, they are unlikely to have entitlement to support from NASS or social services. (In the context of the Hillingdon Judicial Review judgement (August 2003), however, it may be possible for those previously supported under s17 to mount a legal challenge against denial of leaving care support). For most unaccompanied young people, therefore, social services support has ceased at 18 and there has been an expectation that they would make their own way in the world as young adults.

Recent developments in policy and guidance have, however, effected a change in the numbers of unaccompanied young people accommodated under section 20 and in the proportion consequently entitled to leaving care services. Department of Health (2003) guidance on the appropriate use of section 17 accommodation and the findings of the Hillingdon judicial review, in August 2003, have served to create an environment in which entitlement to leaving care support has grown. The increase in demand for leaving care services has been recognised by Government through provision of additional financial resources to those local authorities most affected (Department for Education and Skills, 2004) and there is some evidence of progress being made in the use of section 20 accommodation for older teenagers (Refugee Council, 2005). However, new proposals contained in the Home Office reform programme for unaccompanied asylum seeking children may, if realised, once again reduce entitlement to leaving care services at age 18 (Home Office, 2007).

Preparation

Although local authorities have a duty to prepare looked after young people for adult life, research has consistently pointed to inconsistencies in the preparation they receive and to young people often feeling relatively ill-equipped for life after care (Fletcher, 1993; Biehal et al., 1995; Courtney et al., 2004). What makes for effective preparation is less understood. What evidence there is suggests that preparation should occur gradually over the time young people are looked after and may best take place in the context of a stable placement, where continuity in young people's links and relationships is provided, where education is encouraged and where preparation is formally integrated into child care planning (Stein and Wade, 2000). Guidance to the CLCA, 2000 also emphasises the importance of providing balanced attention to practical and financial skills, interpersonal skills and relationships and health and well-being (Department of Health, 2001).

Providing such environments for young people has proved to be an abiding challenge for the care system. In particular, movement and disruption have figured prominently in the lives of looked after young people (Jackson, 2002) and the educational attainment and post-care economic participation of young people has been consistently poor (Cook, 1994; Biehal et al., 1995; Broad, 1998; Courtney et al., 2005). Recent evidence also suggests that white and mixed origin young people may fare worse in these regards when compared to looked after Caribbean, Asian and African young people (Barn et al., 2005).

At present, we know very little about how unaccompanied young people fare once they become looked after or how their experiences may compare to those of other looked after children. Some (as yet unpublished) fragments of evidence emerging from research studies suggest that they may do quite well. One large-scale study of patterns of placement stability amongst 7399 looked after children has found that, in comparison with other looked after young people, unaccompanied children are less likely to experience placement instability and, according to reports from social workers, are also significantly less likely to display challenging behaviour or emotional disturbance and are significantly more likely to be doing well at school.[1] These findings are also consistent with those from a study (Dixon et al., 2006) on outcomes of leaving care (although some caution is needed in relation to these findings – the study followed a sample of 106 young people leaving the care of seven local authorities, only 12 of whom were unaccompanied young people). This study also found that unaccompanied young people were less likely than other young people to exhibit a range of troublesome behaviours while looked after (including running away, truancy and school exclusion, substance misuse or offending) and were less likely to have had involvement in offending after leaving care.

Furthermore, the York study suggests that the conditions for effective preparation are more likely to be present for unaccompanied young people who become looked after (s20) or who are placed with extended family members than is generally the case for those supported in the community under section 17 arrangements (Wade et al., 2005). The support provided in care or kinship settings brought more consistent engagement with education and stronger networks of social support with family, friends and community. The statutory duties associated with being looked after were also influential. Young people living in care placements or, to a lesser extent, in kinship placements were more likely to have had care plans, regular reviews, regular contact with allocated social workers and broader overall packages of support than were young people living in either supported or unsupported accommodation, mostly under section 17 arrangements. Although preparation for all groups of young people was variable, in these circumstances it seems less likely that important aspects of young people's needs would be overlooked and more likely that the review system could be used to promote a planned approach to preparation.

In overall terms, young people supported under section 17 arrangements fared less well. They were more likely to spend considerable lengths of time out of education and training, were more likely to experience social isolation and to receive inconsistent social work support. However, young people placed in unsupported accommodation from referral onwards were the most likely to have received insufficient (if any) help to prepare for adult life. Many young people had been placed in these settings without an adequate assessment of their ability to manage independently, the quality of accommodation was highly variable and landlords were often unresponsive to young people's requests for help. Patterns of home visiting from social services were often irregular, sometimes non-existent, and young people often had no allocated worker to approach. In these circumstances, young people often felt bereft of professional support and, in relation to life and social skills, often had to rely on a shared process of learning with their peers.

Pathway planning

Transition or pathway planning for unaccompanied young people is a complex task. While all young people have similar needs for consistent information, advice and guidance, the specific duties placed on local authorities vary. Where young people have been looked after (s20), all provisions of the CLCA apply. Where young people have been supported in the community (s17), they do not. However, their need for effective pathway planning to assist them to negotiate these transitions is no less pressing and, arguably, forms part of the general duty to 'safeguard and promote' their welfare.

Pathway planning is made more complicated by the asylum decision-making process. Many unaccompanied young people have approached 18 without a final decision on their asylum claims and, as we have seen, the Home Office position on returning failed asylum seekers has hardened. These factors add significant layers of uncertainty and point to the need for a 'multi-dimensional' approach to transition planning (see also Howarth, 2005; Save the Children, 2005). Multidimensional planning suggests a need for discrete but overlapping strategies of planning and support for several distinctive groups of young people who, though they may have common core needs, may face quite different futures. These include: (a) those with long-term futures in the United Kingdom; (b) those seeking a longer-term future; (c) those who have been refused permission to stay and (d) those who may return to their country of origin. Pathway planning for these groups has to take account of different rights and entitlements (to work and study, to housing and financial support) and, with respect to groups (c) and (d), of the need to prepare and support young people's return. Multidimensional planning therefore needs to be flexible and realistic, taking account of the possible scenarios for each young person, and to develop individual support packages that maximise young people's choices and options.

The York study found that, at least at the time that the fieldwork was undertaken, pathway planning for unaccompanied young people was highly variable. The duty to provide written pathway plans for young people 'eligible' under the CLCA was rarely exercised, even for those who were looked after. Only 3 per cent of young people had a copy of a pathway plan on file, amounting to just 12 per cent of those looked after and aged 16 or over at data collection. This compares unfavourably to evidence relating to citizen young people. Although variations exist between local authorities in the degree to which pathway planning has been implemented, one survey conducted 12–18 months after the legislation was introduced found that 70 per cent of those eligible to have pathway plans were thought to have them in place (Broad, 2003).

Pathway planning provides an opportunity to think into the future with young people, to envisage their life beyond care and to prepare them for different potential outcomes (Department of Health, 2001). The requirement for regular reviews also allows plans to be adjusted in the light of changing circumstances, an important consideration for unaccompanied young people, and provides opportunities for young people to obtain realistic and accessible information and advice. Not only should this process help young people to make more informed decisions about their futures, it may also enhance their sense of control and well-being in the present (Stanley, 2001; Howarth, 2005).

Research on leaving care suggests that the timescales for transition planning have been too short, often compressed into the last few months of care (Biehal et al., 1995; Dixon et al., 2006). Evidence informed guidance suggests that leaving care planning should start early (at least by the age of 16), proceed at a pace acceptable to the young person, involve all those with an interest in supporting them and be based on a well-rounded understanding of their needs and aspirations (Stein and Wade, 2000; Department of Health, 2001). This did not always happen for young people in the York study. Planning was frequently truncated and often took the form of an 'exit plan' for young people at 18. This was especially the case for young people living independently before the age of 18 (whether they had previously been looked after or not) and, to a more variable degree, for those living with relatives or in informal foster settings. A practitioner working in a dedicated agency providing supported housing to older teenagers acknowledged these limitations in their planning process:

> We've got a list of what we've got to do for young people, the basic requirements ...
> It's a six week plan to independence really ... (although) I think six weeks is

optimistic really ... They've got to be independent by 18, that's our aim. (Wade et al., 2005: 200)

Pathway planning should be a gradual process that builds on a positive experience of care. Irrespective of young people's formal service pathways (s20 or s17), evidence of transition planning and practical support was more likely where past patterns of contact with social workers and support workers had been frequent and regular and where formal assessment, planning and review mechanisms were employed to gain a grounded understanding of young people's needs and progress. For some young people supported under section 17, there was evidence of children 'in need' planning meetings being used to plan and monitor their progress towards transition. Social work activity tended to focus on fundamental needs for housing, finance, education and for an immigration decision. However, in some cases, wider issues were also being addressed, including efforts to finalise arrangements for counselling or help to widen young people's informal networks of social support before social services withdrew.

Young people who had spent most of their time in unsupported housing, often with very limited social work support, were the most likely to experience an abrupt transition. In many respects, they were also the least prepared to make their way independently. They were less likely to have participated consistently in education, were likely to have weaker English language skills than other young people and to be more socially isolated. When approaching 18, the arrangements made for them were frequently procedural and minimal. These included notification that social services support would end, referrals to other housing providers or to the National Asylum Support Service (NASS) if they were eligible for NASS support, referrals to Connexions or the Benefits Agency and formal liaison with solicitors if young people were seeking an extension of leave to remain or appealing an earlier negative decision. The degree to which young people were supported through these transitional steps was variable and it was not uncommon for young people to have to navigate a path for themselves.

Pathway planning and immigration

The intersection of childcare and immigration systems at the approach to adulthood makes multidimensional planning necessary. Although few young people in the York study were immune to the risks of an abrupt transition, pathway planning was made easier where young people had leave to remain, which extended for a substantial period beyond 18. Arrangements could readily be made for young people to access benefits, social housing and to ensure continuity of education. A positive asylum decision often lifted a burden from young people and helped to reinforce a belief that they could control their destinies. Young people were able to envisage and make plans for their future.

Where leave to remain was uncertain, this sense of future was inevitably foreshortened. This is where multidimensional planning is essential. The uncertainty experienced by young people was frequently overwhelming; as one young person commented: 'my life is at a standstill waiting for their decision' (Wade et al., 2005: 202). Even though most young people continued purposefully, busying themselves with the pressing demands of the present, others were more fatalistic, feeling that the course of events was largely outside their control. Many identified these anxieties as the most difficult thing in their lives; one that sometimes had adverse consequences for their mental health.

Uncertainty about the future had a negative impact on transition planning. Many practitioners tried to address young people's fears directly, creating flexible plans that tried to connect their needs in the present to the possible scenarios that might lie ahead and to prepare young people, as best they could, to meet these challenges. Others, however, were more reluctant to raise or revisit the implications of a negative asylum outcome out of concern for the further distress it might cause young people.

Planning drift was most likely in relation to the prospect of young people being returned to their countries of origin. Some workers worried about how young people would negotiate such a transition and tried to prepare them for this eventuality as best they could. Time was spent exploring options, identifying links in their home countries that might prove helpful, encouraging young people to consider family tracing where these connections were unknown or partially fragmented. This was not easy work, especially since young people tended to be firmly resistant to the idea of return. For many practitioners, however, the enormity of these questions and the lack of an adequate social work vocabulary to describe them made it difficult to initiate these discussions:

> It's not something I broach really, unless it comes up. Unless somebody brings it up in a conversation first, I don't ask, 'how do you feel about going home?' Sometimes people say, 'I want to stay'. He hasn't said anything like that ... I get the impression that most people in his situation will eventually be returned and it is only a matter of time. (Wade et al., 2005: 204)

Although responses of this kind are perfectly understandable, they are unlikely to be helpful to young people in the long run and can lead to planning drift. Preparation for this eventuality should form one strand of multidimensional planning. Pathway planning needs to be realistic, take place over time and take account of all possible outcomes so that it maximises opportunities for young people to make informed decisions about their lives.

The prospect that more young people may be returned in the future makes it imperative that information is gathered that enables immigration officials to fully assess asylum applications and that claims are well represented (Ayotte and Williamson, 2001). Access to good legal representation has frequently been problematic (Rutter, 2003) but is essential, given evidence that exists of inconsistencies in Home Office procedures and decision-making for

unaccompanied young people (Stanley, 2001). Social workers have an important role to play in arranging solicitors, monitoring the progress of claims, supporting young people through these encounters and advocating on their
behalf. These are tasks that overlay the normal range of duties associated with
social work. Yet, without accurate information about the state of claims, it is
difficult to see how preparation and planning for the future can properly take
place.

Young people had extreme difficulty deciphering the complexities of the
asylum process (as did some practitioners) and were often unable to determine
whether their legal representatives were working effectively on their behalf.
Drift and confusion about the progress of asylum claims were not uncommon
and arose from Home Office inefficiency, the inactivity of solicitors and from
social workers adopting an insufficiently proactive stance. These are matters of
obvious critical importance to young people and, as advocates, social workers
need to view the progress of claims as an integral part of pathway planning.
Where young people lacked sufficient support, delays and errors in the process
were made more likely and transition planning was inevitably impeded.

After care support

From a research perspective, we know very little about how unaccompanied
young people negotiate the journey to adulthood once they reach 18, irrespective of whether they have been looked after (s20) or supported in the
community (s17), nor do we know how they are supported or how their
experiences compare to those of other care leavers (Stanley, 2001; Mitchell,
2003). These are important questions for future research.

It has been estimated that unaccompanied young people who are looked
after (s20) account for around seven per cent of all care leavers in England
(Department for Education and Skills, 2003). However, their concentration
in London and the South East suggests that they will form a higher percentage
of leaving care caseloads in authorities within those areas (Department for
Education and Skills, 2005). Although their knowledge base is extremely limited, fragments of emerging evidence suggest they may fare relatively well on
leaving care, at least in some important respects. National statistics on outcomes for care leavers at age 19 suggest that, for the year 2002–2003, 50 per
cent of formerly looked after unaccompanied young people were participating
in education compared to 21 per cent of all care leavers and 10 per cent were
in higher education compared to just 6 per cent of their peers (Department for
Education and Skills, 2003). Our recent study on leaving care found similar
patterns of education participation and also found that, at follow-up some
12–18 months after leaving care, unaccompanied young people were more
likely than other care leavers to be living in supported accommodation, mostly
shared housing with floating support, and were less likely to be experiencing
difficulties with offending or substance misuse. In general terms, there were

few observable differences in the provision of leaving care services to this group, although options were frequently constrained by the asylum process and they almost inevitably had less access to support from immediate and extended family members (Dixon et al., 2006).

At the time the York study was conducted, however, the vast majority of unaccompanied young people had no formal entitlement to leaving care services beyond their eighteenth birthday. Amongst those who had reached 18 at the close of data collection, most had been supported under section 17 arrangements and for most of this group (77 per cent), social services responsibilities had ended on reaching 18. Case closure was routine and reflected the lack of statutory responsibilities to provide after care support. Continuation of support beyond this point for a (usually short) time was more likely where plans were still being finalised for a young person's transition to independence or to NASS support or where protracted difficulties existed in the asylum application or appeals process. In these circumstances, support sometimes (though not always) continued until these issues were resolved. For this group as a whole, access to further advice or guidance from social services tended to depend on the willingness of social workers to provide informal help:

> I'm sure it is much more about personal feelings and issues than it is professional. But I don't think I'm unique in that. I'm sure there are other workers here who still have contact with young people past 18 (social worker). (Wade et al., 2005: 208)

Many practitioners shared these concerns about young people's continuing need for support and did the best they could, despite the constraints imposed by their formal role and the legal and funding environment that constrained their work.

In overall terms, therefore, the social services departments in the study had formally delimited their leaving care responsibilities to the overwhelming majority of unaccompanied young people in their care. Only a relatively small minority were looked after at this time (19 per cent) and therefore had an unambiguous entitlement to continuing support under the provisions of the CLCA, 2000. However, where looked after young people had moved on to live more independently or to join relatives before the age of 18, arrangements for supporting them were often re-designated from section 20 to section 17 thereby weakening *in practice* (if not in law) their later entitlement to leaving care services. In these circumstances, there was little evidence that transition plans envisaged support continuing beyond the age of 18.

Amongst those who were aged 18 or over at the point of data collection, however, there was evidence of a need for continuing support. Data on young people's circumstances with respect to housing, economic participation and social support was drawn from information recorded on social work case files. Although the CLCA, 2000 places an obligation on local authorities to monitor and report on the progress of care leavers, no such duty exists in relation to those supported under section 17. In consequence, there was considerable

uncertainty about young people's circumstances. For example, it was not possible to discern from case files for quite a large percentage of cases where
young people were living (35 per cent) or whether young people were economically active (45 per cent). Many of these young people had disappeared
from social services' gaze after case closure.

Where information was available, most young people appeared to have
some form of home base. The majority were living in independent housing –
including NASS accommodation, council tenancies and private sector shared
housing of variable quality. Where young people had experienced an abrupt
transition or where they had received a final negative asylum decision, a small
number experienced periods of homelessness, staying with friends and
acquaintances or in homeless hostels. A few young people were discharged
into homelessness and, in these cases, abrupt case closure had generally taken
place before a transfer to NASS or to independent accommodation had been
completed and the barriers presented to young people in negotiating these
transitions had then proved insurmountable.

Information on economic activity and social networks also pointed to continuing support needs. At a minimum, around one in seven young people in this age
group (14 per cent) were not participating in education, training and work and a
substantial minority of the sample had limited networks of support. According to
case file records, almost two-fifths of those aged 18 or over (39 per cent) had no
recorded support at all from family, other adults, friends or community. Other
studies have pointed to the social isolation experienced by many refugee children
and young people (Candappa and Egharevba, 2000; Gosling, 2000; Stanley,
2001). Making one's way in the world at the age of 18 would be difficult enough
for most young people, even for those with close family ties to sustain them. To
expect young people to do so without reliable sources of informal or professional
support is quite unrealistic and reinforces the need for leaving care services to be
available to all unaccompanied young people.

Developing leaving care services

If, as this chapter has contended, leaving care services for unaccompanied
young people have been an area of considerable weakness for social services, it
is important to be mindful of the context of services both at the time the study
was conducted and today. First, the research coincided with the evolution of
specialist children's asylum teams in the participating authorities. These teams
emerged from uncertain beginnings and at a time when social services were
faced with a rapid increase in referrals from a relatively new client group. None
of the local authorities were particularly well positioned to meet these challenges. New policies, procedures and guidance were needed at a time when
there were few signposts to steer the development of services.

Second, planning and support for leaving care represents a moment when
the tensions inherent in the interface between child care and immigration policies

are perhaps at their sharpest. On the one hand, age-related differences in the level of the Home Office special grant that funds work with unaccompanied children has been identified as one factor that has driven policies of supporting older teenagers in the community (s17) and has weakened their entitlement to leaving care support (Stanley, 2001). On the other, leaving care legislation emphasises social inclusion and forward planning for young people into adulthood; policies that are difficult to enact when young people's right to remain in the longer-term is often uncertain. This positions social work practice in territory that is both uncomfortable and uncertain; territory that makes 'multidimensional' pathway planning increasingly essential.

Taken as a whole, these contextual factors help to explain (at least in part) the wide variations in services for unaccompanied young people and the limited engagement with leaving care that this and other studies have identified (Audit Commission, 2000; Stone, 2000; Stanley, 2001; Dennis, 2002; Mitchell, 2003). However, services also develop organically. Over the course of the study, and aided by a downturn in the numbers of young people arriving to seek asylum, the practice of these new children's teams was gradually consolidated and realigned to tighten referral and assessment procedures, to improve placement options for young people (including supported accommodation for those in transition), to reduce reliance on less adequate service providers and to increase the proportion of young people looked after and therefore eligible for leaving care services. These have been welcome developments, prompted and reinforced by Government guidance (Department of Health, 2003) and the wider resonance of the Hillingdon judgement.

Although time will be the final arbiter of these developments, policy guides also carry an assumption that most unaccompanied young people, including those aged 16 or 17 at referral, are likely to become looked after (Department for Education and Skills, 2005; Home Office, 2004; Save the Children, 2005). If this proves to be the case in practice, then the development of pathway planning and of greater consistency in support for unaccompanied young people through transition should be strengthened. Other signals from the Home Office are, however, less positive and new Home Office proposals to reform services for unaccompanied children, including an emphasis on reducing leaving care costs, speedier asylum decision making and earlier returns may, in the course of time, provide a negative counterweight to these developments (Home Office, 2007).

The further growth of leaving care services will also depend on the development of wider resources to create more options and opportunities for young people. Like other care leavers, unaccompanied young people are a heterogeneous group with differing levels of need. The development of resources to provide an improved range of supported housing options, education and training opportunities and initiatives to promote health and well-being will need to address this continuum of needs. It will also require sustained investment, cross-agency collaboration and corporate leadership within local authorities. With respect to these developments, there is much that could be learnt from the experience of mainstream leaving care services. From equally uncertain beginnings, these schemes have gradually gained an expertise and some success in developing resources to support leaving care work, especially in the areas of housing, finance and, albeit to a lesser extent, in education, training and health (see Stein and Wade, 2000; Broad, 2003; Dixon et al., 2006; Hai and Williams, 2004). While leaving care work with unaccompanied young people will always be complicated by the asylum decision-making process, there is a strong core of common ground that should encourage a pooling of expertise and resources. Initiatives of this kind may prove cost effective and help to create a more systematic approach to the development of local authority wide leaving care services.

Note

1. Personal correspondence provided by Professor Ian Sinclair, SWRDU, University of York.

References

Audit Commission, (2000). *Another Country: Implementing Dispersal under the Immigration and Asylum Act*. London: Audit Commission.

Ayotte, W. and Williamson, L. (2001). *Separated Children in the UK: An Overview of the Current Situation*. London: Save the Children.

Barn, R., Andrew, L. and Mantovani, N. (2005). *Life After Care: The Experiences of Young People from Different Ethnic Groups*. York: Joseph Rowntree Foundation.

Biehal, N., Clayden, J., Stein, M. and Wade, J. (1992). *Prepared for Living?* London: National Children's Bureau.

——. (1995). *Moving On: Young People and Leaving Care Schemes*. London: HMSO.

Biehal, N. and Wade, J. (1996). Looking back, looking forward: care leavers, families and change, *Children and Youth Services Review*, 18 (4–5): 425–446.

Broad, B. (1998). *Young People Leaving Care: Life After the Children Act 1989*. London: Jessica Kingsley.

——. (2003). *After the Act: Implementing the Children (Leaving Care) Act 2000*. Leicester: De Montfort University Children and Families Research Unit Monograph, Number 3.

Candappa, M. and Egharevba, I. (2000). *'Extraordinary Childhoods': The Social Lives of Refugee Children*, Children 5–16 Research Briefing Number 5. London: Economic and Social Research Council.

Cheung, Y. and Heath, A. (1994). After care: the education and occupation of adults who have been in care, *Oxford Review of Education*, 20 (3): 361–374.

Children's Legal Centre. (2004). *Care and Support for Unaccompanied Asylum Seeking Children*. Cambridge: The Children's Legal Centre.

——. (2005). Note on Home Office position re Schedule 3 of the Nationality, Immigration and Asylum Act 2002 as it applies to former unaccompanied asylum seeking children, *CLC Information Notes*. Cambridge: The Children's Legal Centre.

Cook, R. (1994). Are we helping foster care youth prepare for their future? *Children and Youth Services Review*, 16 (3–4): 213–229.

Courtney, M., Terrao, S. and Bost, N. (2004). *Midwest Evaluation of the Adult Functioning Of Former Foster Youth: Conditions of Youth Preparing to Leave State Care*. Chicago: Chapin Hall Centre for Children at University of Chicago.

Courtney, M., Dworsky, A., Ruth, G., Keller, T., Havlicek, J. and Bost, N. (2005). *Midwest Evaluation of the Adult Functioning of Former Foster Youth: Outcomes at Age 19*. Chicago: Chapin Hall Centre for Children at University of Chicago.

Dennis, J. (2002). *A Case for Change: How Refugee Children in England are Missing Out*. London: The Children's Society/Save the Children/Refugee Council.

Department for Education and Skills. (2003). *Statistics of Education: Care Leavers, 2002–2003, England, National Statistics Bulletin*. London: Department for Education and Skills.

——. (2004). *Unaccompanied Asylum Seeking Children – Leaving Care Costs 2004/2005 Additional Guidance*. (October 2004). London: Department for Education and Skills.

——. (2005). *Statistics of Education: Children Looked After by Local Authorities Year Ending 31 March 2004, Volume 1: Commentary and National Tables*. London: Department for Education and Skills.

Department of Health. (2001). *Children (Leaving Care) Act 2000: Regulations and Guidance*. London: Department of Health.

——. (2003). Guidance on accommodating children in need and their families. Local Authority Circular, 2 June, LAC, 13. (Available online: http://www.dh.gov.uk/assetRoot/04/01/27/56/04012756.pdf).

Dixon, J., Lee, J., Wade, J., Byford, S. and Weatherley, H. (2006). *Young People Leaving Care: A Study of Costs and Outcomes*, Final Report to the Department of Health. University of York: SWRDU.

Fletcher, B. (1993). *Not just a Name – The Views of Young People in Foster and Residential Care*. London: National Consumer Council/ Who Cares? Trust.

Garnett, L. (1992).*Leaving Care and After*. London: National Children's Bureau.

Gosling, R. (2000). *The Needs of Young Refugees in Lambeth, Southwark and Lewisham*. London: Community Health South London NHS Trust.

Hai, N. and Williams, A. (2004). *Implementing the Children Leaving Care Act 2000: The Experience of Eight London Boroughs*. London: National Children's Bureau.

Heath, T. and Jeffries, R. (2005). *Asylum Statistics United Kingdom 2004*. (Available online: http://www.homeoffice.gov.uk/rds/pdfs05/hosb1305.pdf).

Home Office. (2004). Transition at age 18, *Policy Bulletin, 29*, Version 3.0, 25 February 2004. London: Home Office Immigration and Nationality Directorate.

——. (2007). *Planning Better Outcomes and Support for Unaccompanied Asylum Seeking Children, Consultation Paper*. London: Home Office.

Howarth, R. (2005). *Unaccompanied Refugees and Asylum Seekers Turning 18: A Guide for Social Workers and Other Professionals*. London: Save the Children.

Jackson, S. (2002). Promoting stability and continuity in care away from home. In D. McNeish, T. Newman, and R. Roberts, *What Works for Children?* Buckingham: Open University Press.

Jones, G. (1995). *Leaving Home*. Buckingham: Open University Press.

Marsh, P. and Peel, M. (1999). *Leaving Care in Partnership: Family Involvement with Care Leavers*. London: The Stationery Office.

Mitchell, F. (2003). The social services response to unaccompanied children in England, *Child and Family Social Work*, 8 (3): 179–189.

Refugee Council. (2005). *Ringing the Changes: The Impact of Guidance on the Use of Sections 17 and 20 of the Children Act 1989 to Support Unaccompanied Asylum-Seeking Children*. London: Refugee Council.

Rutter, J. (2003). *Supporting Refugee Children in 21st Century Britain: A Compendium of Essential Information*. Stoke on Trent: Trentham Books.

Save the Children. (2005). *Young Refugees: A Guide to the Rights and Entitlements of Separated Refugee Children*. London: Save the Children.

Stanley, K. (2001). *Cold Comfort: Young Separated Refugees in England*. London: Save the Children.

Stein, M. (2004). *What Works for Young People Leaving Care?* Barkingside: Barnardos.

Stein, M. and Wade, J. (2000). *Helping Care Leavers: Problems and Strategic Responses*. London: Department of Health.

Stone, R. (2000). *Children First and Foremost: Meeting the Needs of Unaccompanied Asylum Seeking Children*. Barkingside: Barnardos.

Wade, J., Mitchell, F. and Baylis, G. (2005). *Unaccompanied Asylum Seeking Children: The Response of Social Work Services*. London: BAAF.

CHAPTER 10

Looking Back, Looking Forward

Selam Kidane

Introduction

This chapter presents and reflects upon the stories of individuals, now adults, who have shared experiences of being unaccompanied children in the past. It draws on the accounts of two young women, Tizita and Naomi, who told me of their experiences, and their stories are linked to my own experiences and reflections on my life as an unaccompanied child. These three stories are woven into accounts already in the public domain, of adults who as children formed part of organised transportations from Spain (Bell, 1996) and Germany (Harris and Oppenheimer, 2000) during the 1930s. The former transportation involved the exodus of 4000 Basque children who fled the Spanish Civil War and the latter involved 10,000 children, known as the Kindertransport, who fled Nazi Germany prior to the outbreak of the Second World War.

Clifford (1997) notes that people who were forced to flee their homeland because of political persecution or war, often maintain an intellectual, cultural and spiritual sense of belonging to their homeland as well as trying to forge a sense of belonging to their countries of refuge. Simultaneously, they look forward and look back in order to resettle effectively. Daniel and Knudsen (1995) suggest that, particularly at the beginning of their refugee experiences, the homeland that they no longer live in is likely to remain a crucial place of emotional attachment, with refugees being 'anchored more to who he or she was than to what she or he has become'. Only after some time can people move on to living ordinary lives in their new lands. So there is a sequence to resettlement. In this chapter, this sequence of negotiating resettlement will be explored with a particular emphasis on the adjustment and adaptation that unaccompanied asylum seeking and refugee children make. The detail and experiences in each of the accounts is connected yet diverse. For example, the people who recount their stories in this chapter lived their lives in different times and political circumstances, and in different geographical, cultural and ethnic contexts. Yet, what struck me as I considered them was that they were all characterised by turbulence and confusion. Feelings of devastation, loneliness, total dependence and loss are a dominant theme amongst the stories here. However, where they vary is in their accounts of how they coped with and adapted to the momentous change that was brought about by exile and separation from their families. Some tell of the ways in which they were able to rebuild and re-root their lives while others tell stories that are marked more by an enduring sense of loss after exile.

Similar stories exist behind every immigration number and social work case file allocated to unaccompanied children who have recently arrived into the United Kingdom. They may hold on to these full stories, folded up inside them for the first few years after arrival, perhaps to be unfolded and shown at a time they can be recounted from a position of safety and security. The silences that predominate for those unable to tell their stories need not be accompanied by feelings of doubt or mistrust by those waiting to hear them (Kohli, 2006). In this chapter, it is hoped that some understanding of the experiences of children who are unaccompanied and seeking asylum in current times may be gained from reflection upon the accounts provided by those who are able to tell and retell their stories from the vantage point of adulthood.

Nothing prepares you for such a loss

My own journey began in 1986. On the 8 December, the sound of a passing train roused me from my sleep in a first floor flat somewhere in Kilburn, North London. Life was never the same again after that morning. On the previous day, I had woken up in my own bed in Addis Ababa, Ethiopia. It had been the hustle and bustle created by my parents and their friends that had disturbed my sleep that morning. They were busy working to prepare me for a journey that would be unlike any other in my life. It was a long day that ended when I collapsed, physically exhausted and emotionally drained, into a bed provided by someone I barely knew. I remember feeling lost and overwhelmed by a sense of being unprepared, as the world that I knew began to fade and another began to take its place. But, then, nothing prepares you for life as unaccompanied refugee child.

Often children and young people are given little or no explanation for their flight. This is perhaps due to a combination of factors – such as, the inherent dangers in flight, the uncertainty surrounding the appropriation of the necessary documentation to enable that flight, and possibly, also the difficulties that parents may find in relating to their child that their safety and protection can only be achieved by separation. Indeed, many of the children that I have spoken to over the years found it difficult to detail how and when they were told of their departure. Some only remember the chaos and confusion that surrounded their departure.

I remember my last day of school in Addis. I attended as usual and did everything as I had done in all of my previous days there. I was anxious about exam results, complained of boring lessons and was almost making plans for weekends that I knew I would never have there. I think I knew that I was about to leave but was too scared to 'internalise' it for fear of being totally overwhelmed by the realisation. My parents must have been in the same situation. On the one hand, they were frantically preparing me for an independent future that hadn't been anticipated to occur for years, but, at the same time, they were treating our separation as temporary, a brief period defined by a time frame. The incongruence was that we never talked about the time frame. This inability to openly acknowledge or discuss what was happening, as the events occurred, is echoed in other accounts.

Tizita, who was born in Addis, Ababa, Ethiopia, was exiled, alone, at the age of ten explains how it happened:

> I remember ... very vividly that the whole thing was something that we just happened to stumble upon and not something that I ... or we all sat down and talked about ... it kind of just happened ... we were going to transit through [the United Kingdom] and my dad decided to go back and I was made to stay here for a little longer and there was a little family complication at that time that I wouldn't want to go into. It was just me without my siblings and I was ten at the time.
>
>   The way the culture works is that kids are never actively involved in decisions and you are in fact lucky if they actually tell you what is going on. ... I don't think I was aware of it [the plan to leave her here in the United Kingdom] ... looking back at the time there wasn't anything that was said to me directly ... it all took place in very few days and so it wasn't a long period of time it all went Bang! Bang! Bang! In fact, it is all muddled up in my head. ... I remember saying goodbye to my parents when they were leaving that was a hug and a kiss and a 'see ya' and really the whole thing hadn't actually sunk in and the effect came much more later than the event itself ... later much later I actually begun to think 'oh my God, so this is what is happening and there is no going back '... no three weeks ... what I thought had a time limit to it, didn't ... the situation didn't hit me until I was actually at the foster placement ... that is where it hit me ... and I was like 'oh my God this is really happening'.

Similar experiences are evident in the narratives of the *Kindertransport* children. Lorraine Allard recalls having four days notice to leave, once her parents had confirmation that the guardians had been found for her in England (Harris and Oppenheimer, 2000: 89). Lore Segal, another of the respondents recalls that at one point her father had said to her that her mother and he could not leave Germany, but that they had decided that she had to go:

> I said, 'what do you mean, I am going to leave?'
> 'You are going to England,' he said.
> 'When?'

'Thursday,' he said.
(Harris and Oppenheimer, 2000: 81)

Bell's (1996) account of the abrupt departure of Basque children from the Spanish Civil War also indicates that they believed their separation was temporary and brief, lasting for a period of three or, at the most, four months. In the end, most remained in the United Kingdom, growing up without ever reconnecting with those they had left behind. Eliseo was 15 years old when he left:

> I didn't want to come. I was crying my heart out. My father took me to the Habana, in Santurce, and on the gang-plank I was still trying to get away. And he said 'Don't be silly. It'll only be for about two or three months, then you will be back.' To sweeten me up he gave me a duro, a five peseta coin, and said, 'Go on. Now get up there.' A silver coin – I've still got it. (Bell, 1996: 44)

The isolation experienced in such situations of enforced separation may be heightened for those who have already experienced the loss of a parent, or parents, or other traumatic experiences prior to exile. This was the case for Naomi, who is Eritrean. She was born to parents in the liberation army and was brought up in a group home with other children of combatants. At the end of the war, most children were collected by their parents but Naomi was not. Her mother had died, and when her father did not collect her, she went to live with his family, where she recalled feeling unwanted and a burden. After a period of time, they decided to send her to the United Kingdom, as there were difficulties for her father who was now a government official. She describes her separation:

> I have never had a close adult person ... even for a year ... every year, every six months ... every something, it is [a] different person ... that is the saddest thing to go without family ... and so when I was told about coming to England that is exactly what I thought ... was I anxious about coming here? ... when my uncle and his business associate told me I was okay ... I was all right ... I was okay ... the problem is I was okay because I was used to it, I was used to it, so I was quite all right but ... I didn't have any family or anything so that part was okay. I never had anybody ... and I have never had anymore contact with my family.

In any culture there are emotional landmarks and timelines that tell members of the community what is most likely going to happen to them next. When children reach a certain age they fall into the patterns of what they have seen others doing. Exile of children particularly the unaccompanied exile of children disrupts this process putting an abrupt stop on what ever was due to occur next. This is perhaps the greatest loss due to separation as an unaccompanied refugee child as their trajectory out from their communities of origin isolates them, shredding any sense of continuity and belonging.

Planning a journey even the shortest of journeys can often be demanding and require detailed preparation. When the one way journey with little or no hope of return, involves a child who is to travel alone without parents or carers, there is likely to be a considerable amount of preparation needed, emotionally as well as practically, for all those involved. Yet, the stories that are known show that many unaccompanied children are seldom prepared for their journeys. They rarely get the opportunity to even say goodbyes to those that they are leaving behind; friends and family that they may never have the opportunity to see again or know about. I remember, before beginning my journey, on my last day at school in Addis, I nearly said '*see you on Monday*' to all my friends but then I remembered that, for me, there wasn't going to be any more Mondays there. But, I could not tell them that either – it was too dangerous. This situation can leave children with many tight knots of feelings, including unresolved mourning and other feelings of loss that never seem to find a natural resolution, delaying an effective healing process. Having disconnected from their origins in these circumstances can leave children feeling disconnected from their new lives, closed off and lonely.

Too unimaginable to comprehend – reflections on early days

For Tizita, it was weeks before she fully realised what had happened to her. She said that it took time for it to 'sink in'. Some of the young people that I have spoken to, say that they would have actively objected to their exile if they had known that it would be open-ended. Others are unable to acknowledge the permanence of their situation, and I have known unaccompanied children who have longed for reconnection over months or even years of their life. In that sense longing has been used as a buffer to keep the shock of the finality of their separation from soaking into them. Tizita described her first few months in London, where a certain sugar rush of excitement gave way to the need to manage loss, in a context of other responsibilities needing to be picked up and attended to:

> My first reaction was 'wow I have got my own bedroom!' But as time went by I begun to miss that whole surrounding I was used to, the people, the community that I was so used to, that was so close to me, which I knew so well but is no longer there. I think that was hard. I had to be a grown up all of a sudden. I had to make sure I had enough to eat and if I don't I know what there is going to be in my lunch box … my little sandwich that isn't going to fill me up. I was learning to do that and that was even harder than actually getting used to the food itself I didn't mind … but it meant having to take responsibility.

Many unaccompanied children express the notion that they had to grow up quickly. I felt this too. My transition to independence was accelerated and demanded a level of maturity that was perhaps out of kilter with what would be usual stages of development. The impulse to explore and experience my new world and newly found 'independence' had to be put on hold while I dealt with the practical demands that it brought. There were many things that needed attention – securing Leave to Remain was at the top of that list. Suddenly, overnight, I went from being a child who did not know how to cross a major road by herself to someone who had to muster enough maturity and strength to negotiate the asylum system and make decisions unlike any that I had ever even considered. I found myself transported from a community that I understood and was understood by to one that was strange and unfathomable. I found myself unable to decode most of the people around me, including the Eritreans and Ethiopians that I came across. I decided that the longer people stayed in the United Kingdom the stranger they became; now, all these years later I often wonder if I appear as strange to newly arrived Eritreans and Ethiopians.

You carry so much in so little – memories and mementos

Inside a jewellery box in my bedroom, there is a watch. It is not a new watch but it is not an antique watch, it was not expensive and it doesn't work anymore. Some might say it is worthless. But, every time I take it in my hands a number of memorable moments are replayed in my mind. The day I was given it by my mother, the time I thought I had broken it three days after I was given it and I had to beg my father to get it fixed for me without telling my mother, and, of course, the day I adjusted it to tell London time. There is so much captured by that little watch, it is a link to my past in my present. But having a memento of this sort is unusual for unaccompanied minors. Many children arrive in their countries of exile with nothing more than the clothes that they are wearing; only sometimes do they bring keepsakes with them. These items are likely to be without value to anyone else but they signify a life that they had, the person that they were and also a connection to the community they belonged to. Some of these items also represent the love that was theirs given by a parent or sibling. Wallela, a young woman whose story is recalled in Kidane (2001), describes the significance and loss of one such item, when the agent that was paid to bring her into the country abandoned her outside a community centre: 'I never thought he wouldn't come back and we left our photo album in his place, that and a little handbag that used to be my mother's was the only thing I had brought with me.'

Tizita did not particularly remember anything that she brought with her but she talked about trying to hold on to memories of her old school, by chatting, many years later, via the internet, to people who had gone there too. For

Naomi, things are perhaps more complex, as the place in which she was raised no longer exists:

> The military camp where I was born and raised is still the place I feel at home inside ... and it is not there anymore because the war is over now [as the fighters returned to their places of birth and the camps were dismantled] ... and it is just mountains there now ... there is nothing there.

Today, I often find myself trying to somehow crystallise memories by collecting mementoes, to capture a moment in a physically accessible way, perhaps to replace those that were taken away when I was removed from the physical space that contains those old memories.

Who cares? – on adults and other carers

Unaccompanied children are heterogeneous – their origins and life experiences vary, they leave their homelands at different ages, take established routes to the country of asylum, or are thrust into unexpected and unplanned entry into territories that they do not know, and cannot anticipate. Yet all have in common their loss of home and their separation from family and friends. That loss is a profound one, similar to yet perhaps deeper than the losses recorded for economic immigrants. For example, Hoffmann (1998: 5) recalls, as a child of an economic migrant family, her departure from Poland to Canada in this way:

> the wonder is what you can make a paradise out of ... I grew up in a lumpen apartment in Cracow, squeezed into three rudimentary rooms with four people, surrounded by squabble, dark political rumblings, memories of wartime suffering, and daily struggle for existence. And yet when it came time to leave, I too, felt I was being pushed out of the happy, safe enclosures of Eden.

For unaccompanied minors it is this move away from home and a niche in a place and people to whom one belongs, that captures the particularly vivid loss of innocence, an expulsion from and idealised sense of living into a grittier, more challenging world. The childhoods of Tizita and Naomi could not have been more different although they come from the same region of the world and were probably fleeing the same conflict, albeit from different ends of it. They both needed support and good parenting to help them overcome their experiences of loss and separation; one found it and the other one did not. Naomi talked about her experiences of being placed within a foster family; she said she did not want to be part of a family and that she still found it difficult to be around families. Naomi felt this because she never had a family, but it may also have to do with the fact that separation meant that she had no opportunity to belong to a family back in her country of origin and no preparation for life with a family over here:

> I was put in a foster family here in London ... and it was terrible ... I was always made to eat outside the house. I lived on takeaway chips almost throughout. Only chips. There was one Ethiopia boy there. He was used to it. He was about 13 then he had been there since he was 8 or nine ... I didn't grow up with spicy food and injera all the time and what my foster carer did was cook once a month and put it in the freezer and that is what we would eat the rest of the month. The same food ... the same food. She wouldn't say hello. She was very scary ... when you go out she never said bye ... Every day she used to call the police on me every single day ... so one day I ran away ... after that there was no way I would go to a family ... no way at all ... they said that I should be with foster family who would teach me and that but I thought I would find it horrible.

Her experience contrasted with Tizita's, who said that she had been woven into the fabric of ordinary family life:

> My foster mother was a Jamaican woman. She had three grown up daughters. We had other foster children but it wasn't a permanent thing, essentially it was the two of us. She [the foster mother] was exactly what I needed ... she was secure with herself, very secure in her surroundings, very strong woman, very caring, very loving but at the same time she would discipline you, she would not take any nonsense ... I knew what time to go to bed I knew what to do. She brought me up well as she would with her own daughters the way she lived and how she related with me I never felt any different from her daughters ... and her daughters interacted with me the way they interacted with each other ... and I was part of the family. I did not feel at any point as if I wasn't.

Foster care, when it is safe and loving, has much to offer separated children – it can provide a home that feels like sanctuary and an adult (or adults) who can act as a parental figure, an advocate, a mentor and a source of support. An adult in this situation needs to be able to make sense of the disrupted narrative so that the child can have healthy attachments in their new world whilst cultivating any links that they have with their parents and networks in their country of origin or elsewhere in the world. Tizita reflected: 'it is a question of who is there for you. I think I had balance. I felt I belonged ... and I am happy'.

Similar experiences – of unaccompanied children needing and valuing a sense of connectedness and being loved – are recorded elsewhere – a testimony to the potential for healing that substitute families can offer. In Harris and Oppenhemier (2000: 130) Vera Gissing, a former Kindertransport child describes her first encounter with her foster carer as she stood alone in a room, frightened, waiting for someone to claim her:

> the door opened, and there stood this little lady ... her hat sat all askew ... and her mackintosh was buttoned up all wrong. She peered at me from behind a big pair of

glasses. ... and she ran to me and hugged me, and spoke to me ... 'you shall be loved'. And those were the most important words any child in a foreign land, away from her family could hear. And loved I was.

So different yet invisible – on school and peer networks

At school back in the homeland, I was an ordinary teenager, getting up to all sorts of mischief but after I arrived in the United Kingdom I began to change. I was different from all the other children. I was a foreigner, although in London, especially in the inner city, that is not such a big deal. I was black, but apart from coming to terms with wider scale racism again, that did not necessarily make me stand out. Yet, my outlook on life, my expectations of others and the responsibilities that I felt I had made me different in an invisible way. I had been given an opportunity that I knew many others had not been given; I felt an enormous sense of responsibility to repay the debt by making something of myself. There was no time to waste, no time to relax, no time to be a child or even a young, carefree person. Years later, I discovered some resonance in the words of a kindertransport child:

> I think I had a sense that when I was lying in bed I was wasting time, that while I was playing, for instance, or while I was laughing, that might be the moment in which I could have and should have been doing something about the demand on me. (Harris and Oppenheimer, 2000: 171)

In their own ways, both Tizita and Naomi also expressed experiencing enormous pressure not to waste time and to do well even when the odds were stacked against them:

> All I remember is I wanted them to be so proud of me. ... Whatever I did and also that I reflected the values and the good upbringing that they brought me up with ... my grandmother was a nurse and so the medical sciences is where I ended up. (Tizita)

For Naomi, in the absence of an immediate family, she wanted to fulfil a legacy for the people who sacrificed themselves for the good of the whole nation. Some were martyred for the cause, she wanted to repay the debt by being a good citizen of a country that she no longer lived in:

> I want to do really, really, well and make Eritrea proud of me, work in the field of development and fulfil the dreams of the fighters who died and who were maimed and whatever I do I know it is nothing next to what they did. (Naomi)

For me, this sense of responsibility created a feeling of difference, which remained ever present but invisible and made it impossible for me to fully join my peers as a 'regular' young person of that age. *Top of the Pops* and glossy teen magazines were the preoccupations of their world, while the BBC World Service's African programmes figured largely in mine as I tried to get a glimpse of what was happening back home. However, this kind of difference is not visible and it does not alert others to the responsibilities that many unaccompanied children feel they are carrying. It may even appear that children and young people are mature or sensible; attributes that are sometimes valued more than they are questioned. I remember a recommendation letter written by the manager of a pharmacy where I worked as a Saturday sales assistant: Selam shows maturity, well beyond her years, she has what I call an old head on such young shoulders.

Permission to belong

Naomi told me about the biggest loss in her life with tears in her eyes – that she has never had an adult in her life who was constant, and when she had the opportunity to live in a family and things went wrong it put her off the idea for good. However, she misses what she never had. Whereas Titza misses her parents, her grandparents and everyone in her extended family, she was able to form a relationship with her second foster carer even after she too had a difficult first placement. In Tizita's case, she feels that her birth parents and extended family, with whom she had maintained contact since departure, helped her to establish a relationship with her foster family enabling her to develop a sense of belonging. She also identified her own personality as playing a part in her ability to maintain her relationships:

> I didn't feel any guilt that I have this emotional bond with my new family that I didn't with them ... they were happy and they expressed that quite clearly and when I did phone they would ask; 'How is your mom doing?' and stuff like that it was no animosity so I didn't feel as if I was torn between two families at all. I think I had balance.

Stability of relationships becomes the scaffolding for laying down layer upon layer of experiences as you negotiate belonging to a new space and with a new set of people. My experience was somewhere between that of Tizita and Naomi. I had a very secure upbringing with lots of positive experiences, but after I arrived in the United Kingdom there were no adults in my life who took on a parental role. However, this gap was filled by a number of individuals who took it upon themselves to provide mentoring, befriending and teaching in their various capacities. They did not really have to do any of the things that they did, but they did them anyway. The kindness of these people still touches my heart so many years later. A year ago I bumped into someone that used to work for the Refugee Council back in the 1980s and as soon as I saw her I recognised her. She was one of those people, she did not exactly remember me but it meant a lot to both of us to link up after many years.

Slowly coming back to life – working towards success and achievements

Last summer, someone made a comment to me about the revival in eighties fashion; I could not, for the life of me, remember what was fashionable in the 1980s or anything else about what was happening at that time. I feel like I gave the whole of the 1980s in London a miss, I was too busy relocating and finding myself in my new surroundings. I do not remember what my political views were and I do not recall much of the music or any of the films or books of the time. Like some of the *Kindertransport* children, I felt for some years that I was 'biding my time, as opposed to living a life' (Harris and Oppenheimer, 2000: 220). The last time I spoke to Naomi, on the phone, she was at work; as an experienced play assistant she is never short of work surrounded by chattering children. In the midst of all the turmoil and void in her life, she managed to build a fulfilling career that she enjoys, but she still has dreams and aspirations to do something even bigger. She said:

> Look, Selam, I am going to make up for all this ... I can't see myself as a parent or anything yet, but I will make it I will make my people proud and I will go back to Africa and be involved in development work.

Tizita also talked about turning things round by making the most of the opportunities that she feels she was given both by her parents and by her foster mother:

> My foster mom was a very strong character; she had me on line. I had a Saturday job, I had to save money, open an account at an early age. I learnt to play the flute, athletics club ... I did enjoy writing. I was given this opportunity to make something of my life and that is what I focused on and did. My parents gave me a good start and that helped me a great deal. If I weren't the person I was at 8 or 9, I wouldn't be the person I am today.

Their endurance and resilience fills me with hope for the many separated children that I have come across in my work. Children like Admass, who was five years old when I saw him last. Just over three years ago, as a foster carer, I agreed to look after a sibling group of two very young unaccompanied asylum seeking children. Their age had made it very difficult to place them, things had gone wrong at their previous foster placement, and the local authority had to find an alternative placement for the children by four o'clock on a Friday afternoon. My husband and I decided to look after them for the weekend but, in the end, they remained living with us for a number of months. Admass and, his sister, Waka always appeared to be living between worlds, afraid of starting a new life for fear of making their loss final. It was as though starting to live life fully would make their severance somehow complete – there would be some invisible point of no return. One particular incident illustrated this to me.

Fights over toys were quite commonplace in our household in those days and in a bid to minimise them, we had bought Admass toys that were similar or identical toys to those of my son (who was slightly younger) so that neither of them would have to share all of the time. It did not work. My son, continued to complain that Admass was taking his toys. On investigating, I discovered that Admass had neatly packed away his toys, some still packaged, in his toy box and was playing with my son's identical toys that he had 'borrowed'. 'You see,' he explained, 'I am saving these toys to play with when we are all gathered together and start living again.' He meant that when his life resumed in the form that he had known to be when he was separated from his parents, his sister, his cousins, his land, his language, his food and his culture.

Unaccompanied children who remain (or are allowed to remain) in the country of their asylum have to deal with not only their past experiences of trauma, loss and separation, but also the social demands of becoming part of their present community. This demand could be complicated by the fact that they often find themselves having to adapt both to the mainstream host community and the diaspora from their country or region of origin. They face the realities of having to make sense of an unfamiliar setting as well as the settings of a community that has already undergone a process of adaptation and hence may be different from that they are familiar with.

I understand but I do not agree

> Our youth, our education, our upbringing – everything we knew – had all been taken away from us. I don't blame the parents. They did what they thought was the best thing for us, what they knew was best for us. The decision was wrong, but they were right to make it.
>
> (Rodolfo, in Bell, 1996: 209)

There are many statements that express similar opinions of those trying to make sense of becoming unaccompanied children. Those whose parents and/or adult carers made the decision often come up with statements that express some understanding if not agreement with the decision. In telling me her story Naomi tracked the difference between understanding why her parents gave her up to strangers, and accepting that it was the right thing to do. It had, she said, put her own wish to be a parent on hold, and that if she ever had a child, she would give it everything it needed, and never let go. She said: 'I would never leave my child like my parents had to when they went to fight. Hopefully those days are over. For my parents it was different. They had no choice. They probably felt the country needed them more than I did.'

There are several testimonies in Bell (1996) and Harris and Oppenhemier (2000) that confirm the vivid consequences of surrendering your children. As the adults reflect on their childhoods and what they would have chosen for themselves, or indeed what they would choose now for their children if they needed to protect them by expelling them from their care, several voices confirm that parents should keep their children whatever the situation. I often look at my own children playing carefree in our garden and wonder if I would ever be able to send them away like my parents had to. I once asked a group of my friends who came to the United Kingdom under similar circumstances what they would do and we found it very difficult to picture such a situation. When my son was Admass's age, I told him about Admass but he was unable to comprehend the story. Although I have talked with friends about some of the complexity inherent in these stories and also introduced my children to some of the ways in which my life has been shaped by these experiences, I have never asked my own parents any questions about any of this. In some senses I feel protective of myself and them. I feel it would be very difficult for me to avoid blaming them for what they thought was the right thing. So for me, like many other people who were unaccompanied children, making the choice about what to say, who to say it to, when to say it, and how, becomes part of the journey of resettlement. In the meantime our stories and the ways in which they coincide and diverge, are told in many voices, through many experiences, spanning many years, but the message remains the same. It is not easy to be a refugee. It is even more difficult to be a refugee child. The experiences of a separated refugee child can at times be so distantly removed from the range of experiences of those that they come across that they are difficult to understand. My experiences and the ones I have chosen to interweave them with show that looking back and looking forward is a process that has depth and complexity, that it is survivable, and that through being resilient and finding people who can comfort you, a sustainable future can be built on the back of a fragmented past.

References

Bell, A. (1996). *Only for Three Months – the Basque Children in Exile.* Norwich: Mousehold Press.

Clifford, J. (1997). *Routes: Travel and Translation in the Late Twentieth Century.* Cambridge, Massachusetts: Harvard University Press.

Daniel, E. and Knudsen, J. (1995). *Mistrusting Refugees.* Berkley and Los Angeles: University of California Press.

Harris, M. J. and Oppenheimer, D. (2000). *Into the Arms of Strangers – Stories of the Kindertransport.* London: Bloomsbury.

Hoffman, E. (1998). *Lost in Translation.* London: Vintage.

Kidane, S. (2001). *'I did not Choose to come here'– Listening to Refugee Children.* London: BAAF.

Kohli, R. K. S. (2006). The sound of silence: listening to what unaccompanied children say and do not say, *British Journal of Social Work*, 36: 707–721.

Conclusion: Dwelling in Possibility

Ravi K. S. Kohli and Fiona Mitchell

Many existing views of practice with unaccompanied children and young people can be limited and limiting. For example, we have noted elsewhere in relation to social work with unaccompanied minors that many research studies

> remain flat and unenthusiastic about ... practice, largely falling into a portrayal of professional ineptitude, having described failing organisational contexts. In their analysis, gaps trump successes, and the established furrow of telling social workers what they have not done, what they have done too little of, and what they ought to do, is firmly followed. (Kohli, 2007: 3)

Yet, in the course of our work as researchers, working separately on different studies, we encountered social workers and other practitioners who had adapted to what they often found to be an intellectually stimulating and an emotionally challenging environment in which to work. Their accounts of practice and policy were rich in detail and unlike the more familiar view within the literature they offered evidence of practitioners acting in humanitarian ways as they made links between 'surface' and 'depth' issues (Howe, 1996), and they said more about how young people begin to take charge of their circumstances over time and of how practitioners could work collaboratively or companionably with them to reconstruct their lives.

The chapters that we commissioned represent subjects that we had continually heard practitioners consider, discuss and wish for an ongoing dialogue on. The puzzles that they continually grappled with in their daily practice, such as their relationship to the stories that surrounded unaccompanied children, the 'clash' they experienced between immigration and welfare systems, the need to communicate and develop relationships across languages, and the challenge of making assessments of needs and risks with limited knowledge and information. The chapters represent different forms of knowledge – including theoretical expositions, reflective accounts of practice and reports on empirical data analysis.

The contributors write within an affirming framework for policy and practice. The impetus for adopting such an approach emerged from a reading of

Parton and O'Byrne's (2000) constructive social work, where:

> it is important to move from a position of objectivism to one of responsibility where
> the worker acknowledges the active role they play in creating a view of the world and
> interpreting it ... the hallmark of ethical practice is that we are reflexive and embark
> on a process, which is mindful, respectful and aims to empower. The ethic of respon-
> sibility positions the worker as a non-expert who tries to open a space for conversa-
> tion whereby the user can actively redefine themselves, their problems and their
> preferred solutions. Dialogue and collaboration are key. The social work values of
> respect, self-determination and working from where the client is, are very consistent
> with such an approach. (183)

In our application, as editors, we are the 'workers' who as 'non-expert' are trying to open a space for conversation whereby, we hope, the user or client, in
this instance, the practitioners or student readers (working with children and
young people who are unaccompanied and seeking asylum) can actively redefine
themselves, their problems and their preferred solutions to the challenges that
they face in their practice.

People have some power and agency, even within oppressive social structures, to shape their own lives and personal consciousness. This is true for
children and young people who are exiled and seeking asylum; it is also true
for practitioners working to help and assist them. Parton and O'Bryne (2000)
state that 'change is not just happening to us; we have some agency over it and
the more sense of personal agency we have the more empowered we are. In
practice this means that knowing what we do that makes a difference is important. Therefore, talking about what is different, about whether what is happening is different or not, about what people do to make a difference, is
central to empowerment' (59). What unites the contributions in this book is
the way in which they identify and amplify personal agency of both the children and young people who are being worked with and of the practitioners
who are working to help them. They do so while taking account of the context
in which lives are lived and practice is practised.

In understanding the forces that shape and can be shaped, what emerges
from the chapters is that the interaction between the outer world of the environment and inner world of the self is critical. This is true for practitioners as
well as for the young people that they are working with. In Chapter 2, Dennis
presents an account of the forces that are experienced as constricting and constraining social work practice but also illuminates how practitioners can maintain a level of agency. Holding onto a sense of agency within a hostile legal and
policy framework connects with Kearney's exposition in Chapter 7 on developing assessment practice within a structure that might be encountered as
obstructive and inflexible. Simmond's assertion that the children's perspectives on what has happened to them will determine how they explain and
understand their story, and potentially their capacity to survive, chimes closely
with the retrospective accounts provided by Kidane in the final chapter. Both

authors speak of endurance on the part of children and young people but also of the importance of encountering people along the way whose hearts and minds are open to loss, distress and the inevitable vulnerability that comes from this.

What is illustrated by various contributions is that constructive interaction between the outer and inner worlds is influenced by human relationships. In the context of the lives of children and young people who are newly arrived into the country, professional relationships are key. Sometimes these may, at least initially, be some of the only opportunities to talk with someone, to be understood and to be accepted. These are themes that emerge from the reflexive accounts on bilingual co-working relationships and on group work provided by Raval and Heaphy et al., respectively. They are also present in the practitioners' perspectives presented by Kohli and the assessment practices described by Mitchell and Kearney. These chapters each speak of ways in which children and young people can be helped to begin to shape their own lives. They also show that practitioners can be responsive on different levels. Their value lies in how children and young people experience them. Such relationships can bolster children and young people's ability to understand, work with and shape the internal and external forces that are integral to change in their lives.

The book as a whole illustrates the potential and possibility of working towards establishing an internal locus of control for both practitioners working in different and difficult contexts and for children and young people who are displaced into potentially hostile environments. In constructive social work, Parton and O'Byrne (2000) posit that establishing an internal locus of control is not only essential for empowerment but also for opening the door to multiple possibilities of change. It is central to the building of durable resolutions. This is the continuing challenge for all those working with unaccompanied children and young people who are seeking asylum within an environment that is in a constant state of flux.

References

Howe, D. (1996). Surface and depth in social work practice. In N. Parton (ed.), *Social Theory, Social Change, and Social Work*. London: Routledge.

Kohli, R. K. S. (2007). *Social Work with Unaccompanied Asylum Seeking Children*. Basingstoke: Palgrave MacMillan.

Parton, N. and O'Byrne, P. (2000). *Constructive Social Work: Towards a New Practice*. Basingstoke: Macmillan.

Index